Teach Your Co

Life is getting more complex and so is technology. Whether it's your computer, a mobile device or the Internet, you need to know the right steps to control technology.

So take the lead and make technology dance to your tune. Loaded with the best tips and the latest advice on products, programs and websites, this book will show you how to be more secure and:

- Protect yourself, your computer and your mobile devices — on and off the Internet

- Control communication overload — email, instant and text messaging as well as cellphone/VoIP calls

- Discover better ways to search the Web to get quality, not quantity

- Find your digital notes, info and files easily and organize your computer

- Make the most of remote and collaborative computing

- Choose and use the right computer and mobile devices

Drawing on 20-plus years' experience each has with technology, husband-and-wife coauthors Don and Susan Silver have teamed up for the first time to share their knowledge after writing 10 books separately. Readers will recognize the Silvers' clear, concise and clever trademark writing style combined with accessible, well organized, up-to-date information.

And the experts agree. Turn the page and start reading the outstanding reviews that *Teach Your Computer to Dance* is getting from *The Wall Street Journal*, *USA TODAY*, computer publications and technology/security authorities around the world.

Complete Cover Quotes on Teach Your Computer to Dance

"I learned something new on almost every page. This book is crammed full of valuable hints and tips on everything from avoiding viruses to partitioning a hard drive."
—Andrew Blackman, Reporter, *The Wall Street Journal*

"I like this book a lot. It's written by people who know what they're talking about and who are up on the latest PC and Internet technologies—and who are able to offer direct advice to those who are ready for technological adventure."
—Jonathan Zittrain, Professor of Internet Governance and Regulation, *Oxford University* and Co-Founder of *Harvard Law School's Berkman Center for Internet & Society*

"*Teach Your Computer to Dance* is chock full of useful tips. You can pick any page at random and find yourself saying, 'That's a good idea.'"
—Andrew Kantor, Technology Columnist, *USA TODAY*

"*Teach Your Computer to Dance* goes beyond simple 'how to' advice. It's a great guide on how your computer can make you more productive."
—Phil Windley, writer of the *Technometria* blog (www.windley.com), Associate Professor of Computer Science at *Brigham Young University* and Contributing Editor, *InfoWorld*

"Highly recommended for *all* computer users, *Teach Your Computer to Dance* is full of practical tips and sound advice presented in an easy-to-read format."
—Suzi Turner, Spyware researcher and consultant, owner of SpywareWarrior.com and writer of the *Spyware Confidential* blog, ZDNet.com

"Great book for the computer genius or novice. Don and Susan Silver provide the reader with clear-cut advice in an easy-to-read style, guiding you through our technology-crazed world. It's a must-have book for people of all professions."
—Rochelle Stewart, Reporter and *Online Living* blogger, *The Boston Herald*

"This book will save you time and money by teaching you better ways to use the full power of your computer. You'll find plenty of tips, tricks and new sites to increase your productivity and decrease your frustration."
—Liz Pulliam Weston, Personal Finance Columnist for *MSN.com*, nationally syndicated columnist (including the *Los Angeles Times*) and author of *Your Credit Score*

"Unlike many computer books, *Teach Your Computer to Dance* is quite easy to read and understand. The tips are very useful and easy to implement."
—Steven D. Strauss, Small Business Columnist, *USATODAY.com* and author of *The Small Business Bible*

"*Teach Your Computer to Dance* is a great resource for anyone who spends time online. Although there are plenty of manuals around on how to work a computer, this is a terrific resource on how to get the *most* out of your computer and online experience and at the same time practice 'safe computing.'"
—Fran Maier, Executive Director and President, TRUSTe

"*Teach Your Computer to Dance* has dozens of expert tips for securing your computing experience. It also contains a ton of great advice for readers of any level."
—Roger A. Grimes, Security Adviser Columnist, *InfoWorld* and author of four books on Windows computer security including *Professional Windows Desktop and Server Hardening*

"The Silvers give you gold with invaluable tips and solutions for using today's technology and keeping you safe from Internet perils. This book is well worth a read."
— Don Taylor, PhD, CFA, Associate Professor of Finance at
   The American College and Advice Columnist, *"Ask Dr. Don,"*
   Bankrate.com

"*Teach Your Computer to Dance* is a pleasure to read. It's a fun, easy-to-use reference book with straightforward, friendly language to cover the what, where and how of computers."
— Charles P. Pfleeger, PhD, CISSP and coauthor of
   Security in Computing

"This book delivers information on a wide range of topics in a clear manner."
— Russell de Pina, Principal, n2active

"*Teach Your Computer to Dance* is well written, well organized and filled with gems."
— Paul and Sarah Edwards, authors of 16 books including *Making Money with Your Computer at Home* and columnists for *Entrepreneur, Costco Connection* and *Homeofficemag.com*

"*Teach Your Computer to Dance* is written in a straightforward, conversational tone that should prove ideal for computing novices without talking down to more experienced users. I especially liked the sections on email security and management which provided detailed steps to help users avoid common mistakes that lead to viruses, spam and potential ID theft."
— Jim Rapoza, Columnist and Labs Director, *eWEEK*

Praise for Other Books
by Don Silver and Susan Silver

Selected Books by Don Silver

The Generation X Money Book

"This is an outstanding book. The book promises tips and it delivers."
—*USAToday.com*

Baby Boomer Retirement

"*Baby Boomer Retirement* is astute and provocative."
— *Los Angeles Times*

Cookin' the Book$

"*Cookin' the Book$* stands alone as one of the funniest and straightforward works on business ethics in corporate America today."
—Peter McGuire Wolf, Ph.D.

The Generation Y Money Book

"Great book. I found the format, with its basic, easy-to-understand narratives extremely well written."
—Cheryl D. Jennings, Ph.D., Gus A. Stavros Center for Economic Education, *Florida State University*

A Parent's Guide to Wills & Trusts

"Excellent book…What also differentiates this book is the writing itself. It is clear. It is concise. It is clever."
—*Los Angeles Times*

Susan Silver's Award-Winning Book
Organized to Be Your Best!
has more than a quarter million copies in print!

"A practical approach to improving organizational skills…a sound how-to, recommended."
—*Booklist*, the *American Library Association* literary review journal

"*Organized to Be Your Best!* is a must read for today's busy career professional. This user-friendly guide is comprehensive in its content and engaging in its style. It is the bible of organization."
—Lee Gardenswartz, Ph.D. and Anita Rowe, Ph.D., coauthors of
   Managing Diversity

"The title of the book says it all. *Organized to Be Your Best!* is the single best resource that I know of for anyone who wants to get more control of their time, computer, paperwork, work space or life in general. It's a state-of-the-art tool kit, resource guide, time management seminar and personal consultant all rolled into one."
—Michael LeBoeuf, Ph.D., Author of *Working Smart* and *How to
   Win Customers and Keep Them for Life*

"Worth a year in college."
—Fred DeLuca, President and Founder, Subway Sandwiches

"*Organized to Be Your Best!* provides unique ideas and solutions that will make a difference in your career."
—Scott G. McNealy, CEO, Sun Microsystems, Inc.

Authors' Bios

Don Silver's greatest strength, whether teaching computer classes at USC or writing business and computer guides, is taking technical, complex information and making it clear, accessible, user-friendly and humorous.

Don writes for the Internet as well as the print world. He has written nine books (including *Baby Boomer Retirement, Cookin' the Book$, A Parent's Guide to Wills & Trusts, The Generation Y Money Book* and two computer guides) and edited 16 personal finance and business books (including four bestsellers).

Don is an educational consultant for *The Wall Street Journal Classroom Edition Teacher Guide,* an online Internet content provider on technical subjects and also a columnist who has written regularly for *Quicken.com* and *Microsoft's MoneyInsider.*

Susan Silver is the recognized organizing expert and author of the award-winning, best-selling business book *Organized to Be Your Best!*—the "bible of organization" with over one-quarter million copies in print. More than ten major book clubs, including two Book-of the-Month clubs, have featured *Organized to Be Your Best!* as a selection. With each succeeding revised edition, this popular book has always featured computer technology solutions.

Susan is president of Positively Organized!—a leading training and development company. With over 20 years' experience, Susan is sought after as a recognized speaker, trainer and consultant specializing in three areas: (1) organization and work management skills; (2) leadership, management and supervision; and (3) business communication skills.

Susan's popular Positively Organized! Programs inspire audiences to be their best by presenting practical tips and tools in a positive, interactive format.

To learn more about Don and Susan, click on www.adams-hall.com.

Teach Your Computer to Dance

Make Your Computer, Mobile Devices and the Internet Perform for You

Don Silver
Susan Silver

Adams-Hall Publishing
Los Angeles

Special thanks to Jeff Butterworth, Stacy Carson, Joe Lee, Robert Rosebrock, Jae Shin and Leon Sterling.

Library of Congress Cataloging-in-Publication Data

Silver, Don
Silver, Susan
  Teach your computer to dance : make your computer, mobile devices and the Internet perform for you / Don Silver and Susan Silver
      p. cm.
  Includes bibliographical references and index.
  ISBN: 0-944708-99-4 (Trade Paper)

1. Microcomputers. I. Title.

  QA76.5.S55145 2006
  004.16 – dc22
                        2005027845

Adams-Hall books are available at special, quantity discounts for bulk purchases, sales promotions, premiums, fund-raising or educational use. For details, contact Adams-Hall Publishing at **800.888.4452 or www.adams-hall.com.**

First printing 2006
Printed in the United States of America
20 19 18 17 16 15 14 13 12 11 10 9 8 7 6 5 4 3 2 1

Aida A. Bahrawy
PO Box 782
Middletown, CA 95461-0782

Contents

Part 4— Dancing Cheek-to-Cheek
Managing Your Computer and Your Info

Part 5—When You Can't Dance Cheek-to-Cheek
Long Distance Computing

Part 6—The Box Step
Finding and Using the Right Equipment

Index

Introduction

The rhythm of life has speeded up. Chances are good that multitasking is your middle name.

Do you:

- Juggle several electronic devices?
- Use multiple email accounts where a good day is just 100 emails?
- Dodge and counterattack spyware and viruses but know there must be more you could be doing to protect yourself?
- Wonder what to do next when your Google search results page shows *only* 1,752,417 websites to check out for the answer?
- Handle phone calls, text messages and instant messages from around the world on a 24x7 time clock?

Whew! No wonder you feel exhausted at the end of the day. Or should we say night?

Finding a Better Way

There has to be a better way…and there is if you know the essential tips, products and solutions to not only control technology but also

1

get the most out of it in the shortest time.

Drawing on the 20-plus years' experience each of us has as computer users and technology researchers as well as Don's longtime experience as an author of computer guides, we've put together the latest and best tips, strategies and products in this new book.

So where does "teaching your computer to dance" come in? At first glance, you wouldn't think technology and dancing have much in common. But whether you're on the keyboard or a dance floor, you can master what at first appears to be too complex and overwhelming. The key is learning the right steps to put you in control.

When you control today's technology, your computer (and mobile devices) will perform for you so you can:

- Protect yourself, your mobile devices and your computer on and off the Internet
- Manage communication overload
- Discover better ways to search the Web to get quality, not quantity
- Find your digital notes, information and files quickly
- Use remote computing and collaborative computing
- Organize your computer
- Identify the right computer and mobile devices for your needs

In this book you'll discover hundreds of key techniques, products and solutions as well as special tips and warnings to keep you a step ahead in the Digital Age. In nearly every chapter, you'll find vital ways to better protect your computer, mobile devices and information. (And as a bonus, check frequently for up-to-the-minute developments at www.adams-hall.com.)

We recommend you make the first three chapters on security required reading. Then zero in on the chapters with the solutions you most need to know right now. So if you're ready to rock, put on your dancing shoes and let's make technology dance to your tune.

Part 1

Don't Let Strangers Cut In

Protecting Yourself and Your Information On and Off the Internet

1

The Dangers Out There

It's a funny world. We go to a dance *hoping* to meet a stranger. We go on the Internet *worrying* about meeting strangers.

As a member of the Digital Age, you need to know security precautions and remedies as well as (and maybe better than) your email, Web searching and software programs.

You need to proactively protect and secure your computer(s) and mobile device(s) to avoid a digital disaster. Because such a disaster is increasingly a real threat and can result in enormous stress, financial loss and identity theft, security is the very first topic of this book.

You need to know strategies and techniques to help prevent or remedy attacks on you, your computer, your mobile devices, your information and your identity — both on and off the Internet. You can't afford to be complacent about security today; you must be vigilant.

Mobile Devices Warning

When we talk about security in this book, be aware that virtually the same issues for computers are present or will be soon for mobile devices, too, as they continue to take on more of the characteristics, capabilities and hardware of computers. The problem is three-fold. First, mobile devices such as smartphones are storing sensitive data such as credit card numbers and contact information and can connect to the Internet. Second, mobile device security attacks are a growing activity of cyber criminals. Finally, mobile devices usually come with fewer built-in security features than computers and the ones that *are* present often are not turned on.

Printer and Photocopier Warning

Often overlooked are some copiers and multifunction printers that have hard drives, email capability and always-on networked connections—just like computers. Data thieves are increasingly targeting such equipment.

So before you send or read your next email, start another Web search or even make your next photocopy, you owe it to yourself, your loved ones, your friends and your colleagues to read on.

Bad News, Good News

The FTC estimates that one out of every 20 adults in the U.S. is a victim of identity theft. Although most identity theft currently occurs off the Internet, the Internet is becoming more of a target for the theft of personal and financial data.

The bad news is that when it comes to keeping your information secure, what you don't know *can* hurt you. If you haven't taken the steps described in the next two chapters, chances are good you probably have hundreds of *spyware* and other *malware* programs on your computer right now such as a *keylogger* and a *Trojan horse* or two (see the Malware section coming up soon in this chapter).

Over the last few years, the trend has moved towards more stealthy malware designed for long-term infections aimed at stealing money and data and away from more visible viruses designed for mischief and getting attention. In other words, we're not just dealing with hackers but with *criminal* hackers who want to steal our passwords, our assets and maybe our identities. *Keyloggers* (programs that log and transmit every keystroke you type including passwords and account numbers) are becoming more widely used by criminals.

Privacy Warning

There are virtually no online activities or services that guarantee absolute privacy. But to give it some perspective, there's no absolute way to keep someone out of your home. That doesn't mean you should throw up your hands and say there's no way you can protect your home. Instead, you should make it difficult, very difficult, for someone to enter your home or your computer without your permission. And you shouldn't leave enticing attractions in plain view in either place.

Wireless Warning

There's a special reason to be concerned if your wireless network is not secure. Some criminals have begun to use unsecured Wi-Fi networks of unsuspecting consumers and businesses to help cover their tracks in cyberspace. Failing to secure a wireless network can allow anyone with a Wi-Fi-enabled computer within about 200 feet or so (even someone driving by — *war driving*) to tap into your Internet connection. Secure your network so you don't face the task of proving to legal authorities that you had nothing to do with criminal activities using your home or business network connection.

The good news is that you can take steps to better protect yourself and your computer and remove unwanted occupants on your computer.

When it comes to your computer and the Internet, you need an extreme degree of certainty that your Internet connection is secure.

You also want to have tools and techniques already in place to cure an infection if and when it occurs. If a tool includes software, make sure the latest version does what you need and is compatible with your hardware, email program and other software. Before you install any new software, it's a good idea to have a current backup of your computer in case the software installation goes awry.

Malware

Computer infections come from *malware* programs that may let hackers see every keystroke (and password) you type and more. Malware is a shortened form of the words ***malicious software*** and it is software such as a virus or Trojan horse that is designed to disrupt, damage or in some way harm computer systems. (Malware is sometimes referred to as *greyware*.) Hackers may get access to all of the data and information on your computer (and maybe your network) and even turn your computer into a *zombie* as part of a *botnet* (secret network) that carries out attacks (or sends spam) to other computers without your knowledge.

There are many kinds of malware. A *virus* is a computer program that spreads through human interaction such as running the infected program. The most common way of getting a virus is by downloading an infected file. A *worm* is like a virus but it is self-replicating and it can spread without human interaction once it's on a computer. A *Trojan horse* looks like a useful program but it isn't. Ordinarily, it is not self-replicating and it does its mischief just on the computer where it's located. Trojan horses are now spreading in ways that resemble virus infections.

Although there is no universally accepted definition of *spyware*, it is generally considered to be (a) any program that monitors your computer activities (such as logging your keystrokes, keeping track of the websites you visit or capturing your personal data) or (b) a program that installs itself without your knowledge or permission. Examples include a *rootkit*, which can install hidden files and user accounts and intercept data, and a *keylogger* (defined a few pages ago).

Protecting Yourself

There is no one magic pill. Because the threats keep changing and don't take just one form, you need a variety of defenses (described in the following chapters) that must be kept up to date to remain effective.

The first step is to make you and your computer a less obvious target. Keep reading for ways to do this on and off the Internet.

2

Lowering Your Profile and Risks

Depending on the situation, you might want to be the center of attention on the dance floor; at other times you may prefer to go unnoticed. Life off the dance floor is like that, too.

When it comes to protecting yourself and your information, your first line of defense is becoming a less visible target by keeping as low a profile as possible. There are many ways to do this.

How to Lower Your Internet Profile

On the Internet, you want ways to make yourself, if not invisible, at least harder to see and find.

Depending on how, when and where you use your computer(s) and mobile devices, take the vital actions explained in this chapter to lower your profile, your risk of identity theft and malware attacks. Be conservative and cautious online whether you're searching the Web or just checking email.

Don't Be Connected All the Time

If you have an always-there, always-on connection to the Internet such as through DSL or a cable modem, you're increasing the chance that someone will find your connection and attack it. Unlike *dial-up* connections where your computer's Internet (IP) address changes with each call, with an always-on *broadband* connection your computer's IP address changes less frequently, if at all.

Tip: Disconnect or Turn Off

That's why it may be smarter to disconnect your high-speed modem or wireless connection when you're not on the Internet or better yet, just turn off your computer when you're away from it.

Read Email as Plain Text

Since malware can hide in HTML code, see if you can set your email program to show email as plain text to reduce your online risks.

Don't Use the Email Preview Pane

Even viewing infected email in your email program's preview pane could cause a problem so shut off your in-box preview pane.

Make Bcc Part of Your Email ABCs

To prevent your email address from becoming part of a circulated list, encourage others to use the *bcc* (blind carbon copy) function in their email program. This allows the sender to email many people in one email but hide their email addresses. This prevents those addresses from being harvested by spammers and at the same time also helps prevent the spread of viruses. In turn, you can use the bcc function to restrict unnecessary broadcasting of email addresses.

Tip: "Reply to All"

Your email program may allow you to disable the "Reply to All" option so recipients can't respond to everyone listed in the hidden bcc field by accidentally (or intentionally) clicking on "Reply to All."

Tip: Bcc Safe List

Because spammers sometimes use the bcc function to send emails, some email programs automatically block bcc's as junk emails. Recipients of your bcc emails may need to add your email address to their *safe list* for your bcc emails to get past their spam filters.

An alternative to using a bcc mass email is sending emails using the mail merge feature, if your email program has this feature, so just one recipient's name appears in the "To" field of each email.

Emails with Either No Subject or "Hi" in the Subject Line May Not Be All That Friendly

Avoid opening emails that have no subject line or one that's too friendly or generic such as "Hi" or "Hello There." This is often a spam email that may inadvertently come from a friend's computer that has been infected with a virus. If you get an email with a suspicious or nonexistent subject line, call or email (without hitting "reply") first to confirm its validity before opening up the email.

Restrict Remote Access and Control

Not everyone needs to have remote access or control of their main computer.

Tip: Limit Access

If your only off-site uses are email and searching the Web, then you don't need to set your computer's controls to allow remote access of your data files and software programs. (For remote access and remote control programs, see Chapter 14.)

Consider Getting a Low-Cost, Dedicated Internet Computer

Computer prices have come way down, to a few hundred dollars for a basic computer box. Maybe it's worth it for you to have another computer, a "search-the-Web computer," that does not have any of your sensitive files on it. That way, if this Web computer gets infected or taken over, you have less at risk.

Don't worry if desk space is a problem. Not only are some new computers just the size of a radio, they can probably *share* your existing monitor (but not a laptop screen), external keyboard and mouse via an inexpensive, easy-to-use *KVM switch*. KVM stands for keyboard, video (monitor) and mouse — see below.

Product Tip: Devices for Multiple Computers Sharing One Monitor, Keyboard and Mouse

The *MiniView Micro USB PLUS KVM switch* by Iogear allows you to share two Windows PCs, two Apple computers or a combination of one Windows PC and one Apple computer. Iogear also has other switches that may be a better fit for your equipment and connections. Iogear, Inc., www.iogear.com

Set Up Your Internet Security and Privacy Levels

Your Internet browser generally lets you select the level of security and privacy you want to have while you're surfing the Net.

Tip: Set Security and Privacy Levels

For example, in Internet Explorer 6 (IE6), you'd do the following:

1. Click *Tools*.

2. Click *Internet Options*.

3. Click *Security*.

4. Select the *Custom Level* option if you want a higher level of security. (You may need help from a techy friend who understands how to select the right options for you on *security level*, *ActiveX*, *scripting*, *downloads* and *trusted sites*.)

Internet Explorer 7 (IE7), the upcoming successor, may have different steps and should have safer default settings.

Tip: Internet Explorer 7

IE7, especially running with Windows Vista (the successor to Windows XP), is expected to be more protective than IE6. For example, IE7 and Vista should let you run the browser in a more restricted mode as a way of limiting damage if the browser's security is compromised. By contrast, currently you're more likely to log on to the Internet using the more powerful Windows' *Administrator Account* where malware can do more damage to your computer.

Don't Go Phishing or Pharming

Phishers try to trick you by sending you an email that looks like it's coming from a known company and then giving you a link to what looks like a legitimate company site. It isn't. It's a fake site designed to get you to divulge personal and sensitive financial information. To avoid this, some bank sites have an image and phrase you preselect that come up each time you log on to the correct site so you know the site isn't fraudulent.

Phishing that's targeted for certain individuals (usually within companies) rather than just anyone is known as *spear phishing*. *Social phishing* is where someone poses as your friend using information you've posted on the Web, often at *social networking websites*.

Tip: Don't Click on Links

The way to have phishers go home empty-handed is to avoid clicking on *any* link in any email. Instead look up the correct Web address on Google or some other search engine and type in the URL (the Web address) of the site yourself.

Product Tip: Antiphishing Toolbar

Netcraft Toolbar helps protect you against phishing attacks. The toolbar blocks you from entering the site if the site is a known phishing site looking to harvest your information and maybe your identity. It also lets you

know (a) how long the site has been monitored (established companies should have had their sites in existence for longer periods of time) and (b) the country where the site is running (if it's not the U.S., that may be a red flag for you). It's available for Internet Explorer and Firefox browsers. Netcraft, Ltd.,
http://toolbar.netcraft.com

At least some phishing protection is or will be built into Internet browsers (including Internet Explorer 7 and Firefox). Also be on the lookout for *security toolbars* that help rate the trustworthiness of email senders.

In another twist, if your computer has been infected, then even if you type in the correct address for a website, you will instead be directed to an imposter website. This is known as *pharming*.

More Secure Sites for Your Sensitive Data

If you provide credit card or other sensitive information over the Internet, try to use a site whose URL starts out *https://* rather than as *http://*. The "s" after http stands for secure. A secure site is designed to encrypt your credit card or other data while it's traveling between your Internet browser and the website's server.

An *https* site should have a *lock icon* in the lower right hand corner of your Internet browser (not on the Web page itself) with the lock in the closed position. Be aware that phishers sometime put a fake lock on a fake site. To test the authenticity of a lock, double left click it to see the security certificate for the site. If no certificate appears, then it's definitely a phishing site. However, even if a certificate does appear, make sure the name of the site and the name under the *Issued To* tab on the certificate match one another.

Unfortunately, there's more to consider if you're not the trusting sort of person. Certificates may be *high assurance* (authenticated) or *low assurance* (unauthenticated). Most Internet browsers currently cannot distinguish between the two types and the lock icon looks the same on both types of sites. That's why you may want a product such as Netcraft Toolbar discussed earlier.

Another protective step is to just use a separate "Internet credit card" with a low credit limit for your online transactions.

Be Careful How You Answer Website Security Questions

Some websites (including nonfinancial websites) require answers to security questions to verify your identity in the future if the need arises.

Warning on Vital Info

Be careful how you answer questions about your mother's maiden name, your birthplace, your birth date or your driver's license number. Correct answers may expose your vital identifying pieces of information to website hackers allowing someone to pose as you for other purposes. Of course, there are certain sites where you want to provide correct information.

Bank websites should have *two-factor authentication* in place by 2007 where you confirm your identity through a password or PIN and also with something in your physical possession such as a hardware token that gives you ever-changing numeric access codes. Some banks already use *computer fingerprinting* where the bank site looks for your computer hard drive serial number to help verify your identity. If you (or someone else) logs on from a different computer, then a more rigorous sign-in procedure is used to verify your identity.

Don't Have an Itchy Clicker Finger

As you maneuver with your Internet browser through the World Wide Web, from time to time you'll see pop-ups or buttons with a message asking you to click them. If you do, you may end up installing a program you'd rather live without.

Tip: Spyware Risk

You may also be unknowingly giving permission to have

spyware installed when you click "I accept" to a licensing agreement (known as an *EULA* — *End User License Agreement*) when new software is installed. Next time, read through the agreement before you agree to its terms and pay particular attention to any references to *third-party* software downloads — that's usually a euphemism for spyware.

"Take Out the Cache" Each Day

The *cache* is a folder that's a temporary storage area for pages and images you've visited. While you're in your browser, get rid of the files and *cookies* (stored in your cache) that you may unknowingly pick up when you surf the Net. If you don't clean the cache, your computer's performance can slow down.

A cookie is a block of text placed on your hard drive by a website when you visit the site. That cookie is then used to identify your computer the next time you access the site. It's a tracer on your hard drive that helps a website remember who you and your computer are. Some cookies do more than this. They also track your movements on the Internet to give marketers a private profile of your interests. Sometimes online sites do it with your permission but some do it without your knowledge or permission.

Tip: How to Clear the Cache

The steps to take out the cache vary with the browser. Some already do it in one step. Internet Explorer 7's *delete browsing history* feature is expected to delete cookies, browsing history, Internet temp files, passwords and form data all at once or one at a time. IE7 is in beta testing at the time this book is being written.

In Internet Explorer 6, you'd do the following 12 steps:

1. Click *Tools*.

2. Click *Internet Options*.

3. Click *Delete Cookies*.

4. Click *OK*.

5. Click *Delete Files*.

6. Click the box for *Delete all offline content*.

7. Click *OK*.

8. Click *Clear History*.

9. Click *OK* to *Are you sure you want Windows to delete your history of visited Web sites?*

10. Click *Yes*.

11. Click *OK*.

12. Click the *x* to exit.

This is probably a good step to do at least once a day. Different browsers have different menu options to perform the same housekeeping tasks.

Be Careful with IM (Instant Messaging)

Instant messaging is not the most secure way of communicating. Although instant messaging can be a great communication tool, it can also be an entry point to harm your computer or your network.

You may want to have a software program to help keep your instant messages confidential and to provide protection against unauthorized IM traffic.

Product Tip: IM Security Program

IMsecure Pro helps secure IM inbound and outbound communications, even across multiple clients. If all parties to an IM conversation are using the program, it is designed to also encrypt all sides of the conversation. Zone Labs, Inc., www.zonelabs.com

Suggestion on Restricting Contacts and Use

Make sure you restrict your IM contacts to just your buddy list. Unless absolutely needed, keep IM simple and disable advanced features as well as file sharing and file transfer features.

Change Your Operating System, Internet Browser and/or Email Program

You may feel what you're using now is too vulnerable. Before you make a change, however, keep four points in mind. First, no operating system, browser or email program is invulnerable. They all have security holes, in differing degrees of severity, from time to time.

Second, it's important to consider not only the frequency and severity of attacks but also the effectiveness of the efforts being made to improve a program or browser's overall security architecture as well as the speed that *patches* (fixes) for security problems are issued.

Third, what is safer today may not be safer tomorrow. If a browser or operating system is more widely used, it's a more attractive target to hackers. But a smaller target can still be a target. As BBC commentator Bill Thompson put it so well, "Security through obscurity is no security at all." And if a less-used browser or operating system increases in popularity, then it may become a more attractive target over time.

Fourth, as security expert Bruce Schneier observed in his book *Secrets and Lies: Digital Security in a Networked World*, "Security is a process, not a product."

The bottom line is whichever operating system, browser or email program you use, what's most important is to regularly (and, if possible, automatically) download security updates and to take the security steps described in this book to help prevent security issues. (For more on browsers, see Chapter 9.)

Restricting Bluetooth Broadcasting

Bluetooth wireless technology is becoming the preferred choice for many wireless connections. However, people are too often unaware of security steps to take to prevent what one article called, "Bluetooth: Security's 'silent killer.'"

Bluetooth offers short-range wireless connectivity (a) to link a variety of devices such as a cellphone and a headset or a computer and a printer and (b) to sync up mobile devices and computers. As with any wireless technology, you need to be thinking about security and remember, absolute security cannot be guaranteed.

How Bluetooth Works

Bluetooth generally has a broadcast range of up to around 30 feet. But the range can be up to 300 feet or sometimes extended up to a mile depending on the device you're using and the equipment a hacker has on hand.

For Bluetooth devices to communicate, they need to first pair with one another. The pairing process occurs not only when a secure connection is established but also when devices are most vulnerable.

You can put your Bluetooth-enabled device in *discoverable (visible) mode* or *nondiscoverable (invisible* or *hidden) mode*. When your device is set to discoverable mode, it is available to pair up with other Bluetooth devices and transmit data back and forth. If a hacker detects a discoverable signal, he can attempt to pair with your device and hack in to steal (or later regenerate) the *PIN (Personal Identification Number* code, also sometimes called a *passkey*) without your knowledge. Even if your device is in nondiscoverable mode, it is still discoverable to any previously paired device — that's a good reason not to accept pairing requests from unknown senders.

The pairing process starts with one user entering a PIN, which is used to generate a link key. This initial exchange between devices occurs over an unencrypted link so it's vulnerable. The link key can be stored in the device's memory to authenticate and authorize the devices when they connect up again in the future. Once devices are paired, they have full access to the shared services on the other device.

The Dangers of Bluetooth

There are six main ways a hacker can attack your Bluetooth device:

1. By *bluebugging,* hackers can eavesdrop on your telephone conversations as well as make calls, send and receive text messages and access the Internet on your phone. Some mobile devices are susceptible to bluebugging but not bluesnarfing (see next item).

2. Through *bluesnarfing,* hackers may be able to access your mobile device's data (including contact information) without your knowledge. Generally, newer devices block bluesnarfing.

3. With *bluejacking,* business cards are sent anonymously to your Bluetooth device trying to get you to add the sending device to your address book. Don't do it. If your device is set to a nondiscoverable mode, bluejackers shouldn't be able to find you.

4. *Bluesniping* is when a hacker uses a laptop and a powerful antenna to extend the broadcast range.

5. Mobile viruses can spread via Bluetooth to your devices. Your mobile device could then transmit a virus to your computer via synchronization.

6. With cars starting to use Bluetooth, a hacker can use software to send and receive audio from a Bluetooth connection in your car.

19 Ways to Better Protect Yourself When Using Bluetooth

You'll want to take special precautions when using Bluetooth:

1. Lower your presence by keeping Bluetooth turned off when you're not using it.

2. In general, when Bluetooth is on, keep your device in the nondiscoverable (hidden) mode rather than the visible mode. Read the Bluetooth portion of your device's manual so you know how to make your device invisible and turn Bluetooth off.

3. Since devices in discoverable mode often have a default name, change the name to something anonymous.

4. Once paired, go to nondiscoverable mode. This invisibility will not affect that pairing.

5. Pair devices in private.

6. If devices become unpaired in public, go to a private location to pair them again.

7. Don't pair with unknown users or devices.

8. Don't accept files from unknown or suspicious senders.

9. Periodically look on your device at the stored list of paired devices to make sure only invited devices are included.

10. Use a long, complex and not easily guessed Personal Identification Number (PIN) code when pairing devices. PINs are four or more character alphanumeric codes. A total of eight to 16 letters and numbers is recommended. The longer the PIN, the harder it is to crack. Some devices are manufactured with only a four-character limit which is very vulnerable.

11. Change default passwords for wireless headsets.

12. Use built-in security features that only let authorized devices (e.g., your mobile device and your computer) communicate with one another.

13. Use encryption when connecting with a computer.

14. Use combination keys as link keys rather than unit keys for better security.

15. Install antivirus software on your mobile devices.

Product Tips: Mobile Device Malware Protection

For software to help protect against mobile device malware threats, contact:

      F-Secure Corp., www.f-secure.com

      McAfee, Inc., www.mcafee.com

16. Periodically check the device manufacturer's website for security patches and updates.

17. Don't store sensitive data such as credit card numbers, your Social Security number or passwords on any wireless device.

18. If you lose your Bluetooth device or it's stolen, make sure the previously paired devices unpair your device so the lost or stolen device can't access the services of the paired devices that are within the broadcast range.

19. Avoid using Bluetooth during meetings. Bluetooth is sometimes used to create a temporary computer network during meetings so files can be shared among computer users. Because there is no built-in security with this type of sharing arrangement, someone out of sight but within range (potentially up to 300 feet away or more) could link up with the networked computers to capture data.

The best advice is avoid using Bluetooth in very public settings such as airports and trains and use the invisibility and other security settings whenever possible.

Passwords

Although it's a pain to come up with and keep track of different passwords and to change them on a regular basis, you're just asking for trouble if you don't carefully manage your passwords.

Select Passwords Carefully

These days, to restrict access to your computer and your files, you can have fingerprint, retinal or facial information scanning.

But if you're like most of us, passwords are your primary way of restricting improper use of your identity, your computer and your mobile devices. It's important to give some thought and use some imagination in setting up your passwords. In general, if your password is easy to remember, it's also easy to crack.

Warning on Password Crackers

There are software programs known as *password crackers* that can easily decipher primitive passwords.

Tips: Password Creation

Use more complex passwords (a combination of *at least* eight to ten upper and lowercase letters, numbers *and* keyboard symbols) to give greater security to your passwords. As passwords increase in length, they become more secure because the number of possible combinations to try to crack them goes up, too.

Have at least one symbol character in the second through sixth positions. Make each password significantly different from prior passwords. Passwords should not contain real words, actual names, addresses, phone numbers or birth dates. Change your passwords at least several times a year. Use different passwords for different websites and programs.

A login password when you start your computer may not be enough security. You may also want to set up passwords before your screen saver, hibernation or standby mode lets you (or someone else) resume work at the screen. These types of passwords help protect you if you walk away from your turned-on computer for even a few moments and leave it otherwise unprotected from passersby.

Be on the lookout for two trends in password security. First, graphical passwords are being developed where you select areas on your computer's screen or click points in an onscreen picture you preselected or click on certain icons instead of typing in a password. Second, onscreen keypads where you click on keys using your mouse to enter in PINs are being used to thwart keystroke logging malware.

Store Passwords Securely

Although there are many password manager programs (to track and store all of your passwords) that get good reviews from independent sources touting them as a secure way to store your online passwords, we still worry about having all of your passwords in one place on your computer. Although there are password technologies including *password synchronization, single sign-on (SSO)* and portable, encrypted *password tokens,* we prefer keeping our passwords *off* our computers as handwritten hard copy in a secret place.

Tips: Passwords, InfoCards and Project Higgins

InfoCards — a new form of identity management designed by Microsoft to replace passwords and login names — use a mutual authentication technology that requires both the consumer and the destination site to positively identify one another. Another system, code-named *Project Higgins,* based on a concept developed by Harvard Law School's Berkman Center for Internet & Society, is being designed to give consumers more control over their online identity information. Neither system is out at the time this book is being written so it's too early to tell how they'll each work in the real virtual world.

Restrict Automatic Password Completion

There are two kinds of *AutoComplete* where your computer automatically types in information once you start to type. You probably want to keep the first kind — automatic completion of Web addresses you start to type in.

But you may *not* want to keep the second — having your passwords automatically typed in at websites. If that's the case, change the AutoComplete settings. This will also give you more protection if you lose your computer or someone else gets hold of it. Besides disabling AutoComplete, you can also delete all the passwords that are stored on your computer.

Tip: How to Turn Off AutoComplete and Delete Passwords

If you're using Internet Explorer 6 (the successor Internet

Explorer 7 is expected to simplify the steps) and want to keep your passwords more private, here are the steps:

1. Click *Tools*.

2. Click *Internet Options*.

3. Click the *Content* tab.

4. Click the *AutoComplete* button.

5. Uncheck *User Names* and *Passwords on Forms* if any checkmarks appear (if you don't want forms filled in automatically, then uncheck *Forms* here, too).

6. Click *Clear Passwords* (if you want the forms cleared, then click *Clear Forms*, too).

7. Click *OK*.

8. Click *OK* again.

File Sharing and Access to Information

File sharing and access isn't always intentional. Read on to see ways to tighten up how you handle these issues.

Limit Your File Sharing

Your computer may be on a home or work network where files or folders are shared.

Check to see which of your files and folders you're sharing through your operating system and whether you really need to share them. Restrict unnecessary file and folder sharing so if one computer on a network gets infected, the rest of the computers on the network are less likely to catch the bug.

Remove Metadata Before Sharing Files

A word processing, spreadsheet or presentation file you create may contain *metadata* (hidden information) that you may not want to share when you email someone a file or provide a CD, DVD or disk. This metadata is not immediately apparent when you view the document.

Metadata in a document can include:

1. Your name and the names of previous document authors

2. Your company's name

3. The name of your computer and the network server or hard disk where the file was saved

4. The location of the file on your computer

5. Document revisions and versions

6. Template information

7. Hidden text or cells and nonvisible portions of embedded OLE objects

8. Comments

Risks/Embarrassments with Metadata

What's the problem with distributing a spreadsheet, word processing, presentation or other file to customers, clients or coworkers containing metadata that hasn't been removed?

Warning on Others Seeing Metadata

Computer-savvy recipients will be able to see the hidden data in your files. So, for example, if you are "recycling" a document, agreement or presentation from a prior client for a new client, your new client may not only discover the old client's name and information that's hidden in the new document but also see what was modified (or wasn't) and how much (or little) work was involved in preparing the revised document. That's probably not what you intended to happen and may also violate confidentiality obligations toward the old client.

Product Tip: Metadata Removal Program

With the free Microsoft Office add-in, *rhdtool.exe*, you can permanently remove the hidden data and collaboration data from the Windows XP 2002 and 2003 versions of

Word, Excel and PowerPoint. Go to www.microsoft.com and search for *rhdtool.exe*. For more information on metadata, go to http://support.microsoft.com and search for *223396*.

Metadata Cover-up Is Not Removal

And if you really intend to delete metadata, make sure you don't just cover it up. For example, on documents converted from a Word file into a PDF, techniques such as covering text with black (putting black boxes on top of digital text) or adding graphics on top of existing graphics don't hide or delete what you want removed.

Make Metadata Intentional

Metadata can be useful. For example, Windows Vista is expected to use metadata along with keywords and comments to allow better searching, grouping and sorting of files.

With metadata being more emphasized, remembering to remove metadata may be more of an issue in Windows Vista but the *Document Inspector* options are expected to let you more easily remove metadata. It's important for you to only share metadata where it's an intentional act on your part.

Product Tip: See Hidden Formatting in Word

Speaking of hidden data, you may want to get better control of the hidden formatting in your Word documents. With the software program *Crosseyes*, you can see the hidden formatting codes in Word similar to what WordPerfect shows. Levit & James, Inc., www.levitjames.com

Permanently Erase Files

When you delete files from your computer, those files may not, in fact, be gone. That can be a problem when you sell or donate your computer or when you use someone else's computer to create and then delete those files. Since it's often possible to restore those so-called "deleted files," you may be unintentionally providing access to those files and your information.

Tip: Removing Traces and Overwriting Files

To better protect your files, use a trace-removing program. Some programs substitute random characters to overwrite files that are deleted and others take protection a step further by overwriting all unused hard disk space for additional undeletion protection. (Also see stealth USB drives later in this chapter.)

Product Tips: Trace Remover Programs

BCWipe is designed to securely delete files from disks so recovery by any means is impossible. BCWipe is fully integrated into the Windows shell. Jetico, Inc., www.jetico.com

Window Washer removes data on your Web and desktop activities. For deleted computer files, the program is set up to completely overwrite the files with random characters making them permanently unrecoverable by undelete or unerase utilities — a security feature that exceeds the tough standards of the Department of Defense and the National Security Agency. Webroot Software, Inc., 866/612-4227 [CO] or www.webroot.com

Also see Chapter 18 for tips on removing data from mobile devices.

Handle Attachments Cautiously

In general, avoid opening up files attached to emails or IM from senders you do not know. Those files are a great way to infect your computer. Use your common sense — if an email or IM looks or smells like trouble or you have an uneasy feeling, don't open it up.

Warning on Opening Attachments

But even if you receive an attached file from a person you do know, don't download or open up a file that has an extension (i.e., ends with) *exe* in the name. Also, don't open or download files with two extensions.

Tip: Unusual Email Subject Lines

If you start receiving emails with unusual subject lines from people you know, call the sender to confirm whether they sent it or malware did.

Tip: Virus-Scan All Attachments

And of course, always do a virus scan on any attachment before opening it up.

Use a File Viewer Program

You may also want to use a file viewer program so you can see the contents of a file such as an attachment to an email without opening up the file. Since opening up an attachment is one of the main ways to get viruses and worms, this type of program helps protect you by allowing you to look at what's in a file without really opening it up.

Product Tip: File Viewer

Quick View Plus is designed to allow you to see the contents of a file without opening it up and being exposed to any viruses or worms inside the file. Avantstar, Inc., 877/829-7325 [MN] or www.avantstar.com

Security Issues with Desktop Search Programs

A desktop search program (see also Chapter 11) allows you to quickly search for virtually anything on your computer. This type of instant search program may also allow *anyone else* to discover your information if they can get access to your computer in person or online (such as via hacking) for even a few seconds.

Because these search programs are instant finding programs, a search on your computer, for example, for "Social Security Number" could quickly turn up every place it appears on your computer's hard disk. To help prevent problems, have password protection or more sophisticated authentication procedures in place to operate your computer.

Tip: Maintaining Privacy

With some desktop search programs, if users use separate Windows accounts (different usernames to log in), there are privacy options to encrypt the index so one user will not be able to access another user's desktop search index. You may also be able to limit access to specified folders.

Warning: Multiple Computer Searching

If you're using one of the second-generation desktop search programs that can also search across multiple computers, you might want to keep this multi-computer search feature turned off entirely or at least specify that certain sensitive files or folders (including specific email folders) not be shared among the computers. These programs may have separate consumer and *enterprise* (business) versions. Only the enterprise version may give management tools to centrally control whether the multiple computer search feature is turned on or off on each linked computer.

Be aware, too, the search engine company may copy and store your data (for a limited or possibly an indefinite period of time) on the search engine's servers. Whenever a copy of your data is in the hands of someone else for any period of time, the chances of that data being used, released or subpoenaed go up.

Security Issues with Search Engines

Search engines may store your search history forever. The good news is that your search history is generally tied to your computer but not to your name. However, your name and search history can be linked together. How? If you use a search engine and also another service offered by that search engine company (e.g., email account, online groups or online photo storage), then the company may have your name, address and other kinds of *personally identifiable information* (*PII*) about you which they could link up with your search history. Is this *1984* or just part of modern day life? You decide.

In any event, all of this collected information could possibly become available not only to hackers if they penetrated search engine security defenses but also to the government and maybe even to litigants in divorces through subpoenas. Products such as *Anonymous Surfing* (www.anonymizer.com) can help protect the privacy of Internet searches if all of its encrypting and hiding features are used.

Leaving No Traces While Out

If you're handling email, instant messages and Web searches outside your office, protect yourself wherever you're using your computer or mobile devices.

Keep from Getting Burned at Hot Spots

You may use a wireless (e.g., Wi-Fi) connection at a hot spot (e.g., coffee shop or hotel) or even a wired network connection (e.g., at some hotels) to connect to the Internet. Some hot spots have better security protection than others. Be aware that even wired connections can be "sniffable" where *sniffer* software can penetrate the defenses of the network. That's why as a first line of defense, try to minimize your use of hot spots, especially if you're dealing with sensitive information.

And there is another concern at Wi-Fi hot spots. You may encounter *evil twins*—illegitimate wireless networks that appear to be trusted Wi-Fi connections to the Internet. Here's how this scam works: an attacker positions himself by a Wi-Fi access point such as a coffee shop and broadcasts his own imposter signal (as the evil twin) to get you to log on to his network and reveal your passwords, credit card numbers and other personal information.

Try not to use instant messaging at hot spots since this is not the most secure method of communicating. And if you must use a hot spot, turn off your wireless card when not in use.

Warning on Wi-Fi Networks

Wi-Fi is a wireless shared network often found in airports and coffee shops. Fellow customers may be more interested in the information on your computer than a caffeine buzz. With their Wi-Fi equipped laptop computers, they may be trying to monitor all of your online

activities to capture your confidential information, passwords and credit card information.

Another protective step is to get a program that erases your passwords, temp files and surfing history from a Net session.

Product Tips: Internet Privacy and Trace-Removing Software

Acronis Privacy Expert Suite is designed to remove traces
of your Internet activity, shred files on your computer
you don't want recovered and be real-time antispyware.
Acronis, Inc., www.acronis.com

Anonymous Surfing is designed to shield your IP address
and protect you from online tracking, pharming attacks
and snoops with its always-on 128-bit SSL (Secure Socket
Layer) encryption. The goal is to let only your computer
view any data being sent to or from it over a wireless or
wired connection, especially when you're in public places
such as the local coffee shop. It works silently in the background, without slowing down your Internet connection.
Anonymizer, Inc., www.anonymizer.com

GhostSurf is a very useful Net surfing tool designed to
provide an anonymous, encrypted Internet connection
and erase traces of your surfing. Tenebril, Inc., 800/790-
9060 [CA] or www.tenebril.com

Use a VPN for the Best Protection

The most protective step you can take at hot spots is to use a *VPN*
(Virtual Private Network). A VPN is designed to create a secure,
encrypted private *tunnel* when using the very public Internet. It can
offer security similar to an https site. This can help protect not only
your email (check for compatibility with your email program) but
also all of your other Web traffic.

Product Tips: VPN Solutions

HotSpotVPN is a VPN service that offers two encryption
levels. HotSpot VPN-1 uses 128-bit SSL protection and

can also work with Palm and Pocket PC devices. HotSpot VPN-2 comes in three flavors with up to 256-bit encryption. WiFiConsulting, Inc., www.hotspotvpn.com

Total Net Shield is designed to encrypt all of your Web communications by creating an encrypted virtual tunnel (VPN) to and from your computer. Anonymizer, Inc., www.anonymizer.com

If you're connecting to a corporate network, also use a VPN so your connection is more secure.

Product Tip: Portable Virtual Private Network

Realm iD3 Personal Server is a device the size of a small cellphone that lets you use applications and services on a corporate network from any host PC via a USB port (regardless of the operating system) without installing new software or requiring a system reboot. It sets itself as a VPN (virtual private network) client so there is additional security and less risk of being exposed to spyware, keyloggers and viruses. Realm Systems, www.realmsys.com

Email at Hot Spots

If you're not using a VPN, both your email login password and your emails may be vulnerable at hot spots unless you use some kind of secure connection.

When you check email at a hot spot, you're either using a Web-based account (e.g., Google's Gmail) or an email program (e.g., Outlook).

Web-based account

If you use a Web account to handle email, you can have a more secure login to protect your password by going to a login Web page that starts out as *https://* rather than as *http://*. The "s" stands for secure. Using a secure site to log in for your email keeps your password safer. However, you may then be redirected to a regular http site to read and send emails. Find out whether you automatically stay on a secure site after logging in to protect the privacy of your email reading and sending. If not, see whether you can take steps to get more complete protection. For example, if you're using the Firefox browser and Google's Gmail, you could install the Customize Google extension (add-on) at *http://customizegoogle.com*. This would let you redirect email to a more secure site, *https://gmail.google.com*.

Email program

If you're using an email program (e.g., Outlook) to check email at a hotspot with your ISP (Internet Service Provider), rather than the hot spot's ISP, see whether your ISP or email program offers a secure connection for checking email (*secure POP3* or *secure IMAP*) or sending it (*secure STMP*). However, if you must use the hotspot's ISP to connect to the Internet, it may not be that secure. That's where a Web-based email service such as the secure connection for Gmail discussed above may be the safer way to go at a hot spot if you don't use a VPN.

Turn Your USB Drive into a Stealth Drive

If you're traveling light and just bringing along a portable USB drive with essential files rather than your laptop, be aware that plugging these drives into someone else's computer has the risk of leaving traces of your data on the host computer. Look for USB drives or software specially designed to prevent this from happening.

Product Tip: USB Drive Protection Software

P.I. Protector Mobility Suite software, loaded on a USB flash drive, creates a portable computing environment providing access to a wide range of applications such as private Internet browsing, portable Outlook email, portable Outlook Express email and file synchronization. With P.I. Protector software, when you search the Web or just access your email, the product is designed to maintain your privacy by diverting your Internet activities to the flash drive and leaving no trace of your activities on the computer hard drive. P.I. Protector does not require installation or additional set up on the host computer. Imagine LAN, Inc., 800/372-9776 [NH] or www.imaginelan.com

Product Tips: Protected USB Drives

The *M-Trust Drive* is designed to allow mobile professionals to securely store sensitive information. It has strong hardware encryption and complex password protection and can even be set to self-destruct after too many wrong password attempts. M-Systems, Ltd., 408/470-4440 [CA] or www.m-systems.com

U3 provides the platform for the creation of USB smart drives and smart applications. U3 smart drives hold not only data and files but also U3 software applications. This means that you can carry your personal workspace and use it on any PC wherever you go. U3 LLC, www.u3.com

Malware Warning

Since plugging a USB drive into a computer may pick up malware, you'll want to arm your USB with some antispyware (such as *AdAware*, www.lavasoftusa.com) and antivirus software (such as *AntiVir Personal Edition Classic*, AntiVir Personal Products, GmbH, www.free-av.com) that don't take up too much space on the flash drive. (See Chapter 3 for more information on antispyware and antivirus software.)

Warning: Security Risks to Your Computer

On the other side of the coin, be aware that anyone who connects up a USB drive, MP3 player, PC card, Wi-Fi, Bluetooth or Firewire device to *your* computer may get complete access to (and make a complete copy of) your computer's contents (*pod-slurping*) if safeguards aren't in place.

Get a Privacy Filter for Your Monitor

Useful for traveling, a privacy filter prevents fellow passengers on a plane or train from seeing what's on your computer screen.

Prevent Theft

Take steps to prevent theft of your laptop or desktop computer as well as your mobile devices. You can lock up or tether computers of any size to a desk; have an alarm installed on your computer; and install tracking software that will call or email a tracking station when your computer has been taken or even delete or encrypt files of the missing computer. On the road, make your laptop computer more inconspicuous by using a backpack rather than a laptop case to carry it. As for a mobile device, never leave it sitting in an office cubicle while going off to lunch or a meeting.

Product Tips: Tracking Software

CyberAngel Security Software silently transmits an alert to a security monitoring center if authentication is breached at login or boot-up. The software identifies the location from which a computer is calling. CyberAngel Security Solutions, Inc., 800/501-4344 [TN] or www.sentryinc.com

Stealth Signal software secretly sends a signal via telephone or an Internet connection allowing Stealth Signal to track your computer's location when you report it as lost or stolen. In addition, this software can delete files remotely. Computer Security Products, Inc., www.computersecurity.com

Routers

Routers do more than allow several computers to access the same Internet connection simultaneously; they can also provide protection for your computer against viruses, worms and other malware.

Install a Router with a Built-in Hardware Firewall

If this lingo makes you feel lost already, stick around. This is important information and you'll get the gist of it in just a few paragraphs. A *router* is a piece of hardware. Your computer's modem gets plugged into it. A router that's part of your Internet connection acts just like a high fence that's around your home. Just like a fence, it can make it more difficult for a stranger to see what's behind the barrier (your computer) and to go after what's being protected.

Some fences are more protective, completely concealing what's hidden behind them. Routers are like that, too.

Although a router is ordinarily used with a computer network to connect up several computers to the Internet, you can (and should) use a router with even one computer.

Here's why. Every computer uses an address known as an IP (Internet Protocol) address to connect to the Internet. A router with built-in NAT (Network Address Translation) helps hide the IP address of your computer and that makes it tougher or impossible for hackers to find your computer. Outsiders see the IP address of your router, but not the IP addresses of the computers connected to the router. It's like a burglar looking on a map for your house but your house number is unlisted.

A router can give you extra protection by having a built-in *hardware firewall*. If your router is like a fence around your home, a hardware firewall is like a bouncer at the front door who decides who comes in. You'll also want to have a *software firewall*, too, as you'll see in Chapter 3. Some software firewalls help control not only incoming traffic to your computer but outgoing traffic, too. Make sure you keep your "human firewall" turned on, too, by staying vigilant and careful.

Make Your Router More Secure
Since you can adjust the settings on a router to make it more protective, use the most secure ones.

Tip: Use Stateful Packet Inspection
For a more secure firewall architecture, use a router that has Stateful Packet Inspection.

Tip: Have a VPN Endpoint Router
Some routers have a built-in *VPN endpoint* that makes it easier to set up a VPN.

Change the Password on Your Router
Routers have a preset factory installed password to allow modifications to the router's settings.

Tip: Change Factory Default Passwords

Change the factory default password to maintain control over your router; otherwise, a hacker who can find your router may be able to get control of it by typing in the factory-installed password and then do a router rooter job on your computer.

Disable Remote Control of Your Router

If your router's settings allow remote management, your computer could be attacked. Disable the remote management setting unless this is absolutely needed.

Wireless Routers and Networks

Wireless connections can give you great freedom but as Thomas Jefferson said, "The price of freedom is eternal vigilance."

Our feeling is that it is worth the money to get professional help to set up a more secure wireless network (especially if the following information is foreign to you).

Keep in mind that your Wi-Fi may use the same technology as 2.4-GHz (gigahertz) cordless phones. To minimize interference, keep your phone base and wireless access points apart. Also make sure your microwave oven, cordless phones, baby monitors and halogen lamps aren't too close to cause interference. You may need to change the Wi-Fi signal channel from the default. Better yet, see if you can get Wi-Fi equipment that uses the 5.8 GHz frequency rather than the more crowded 2.4 GHz frequency.

Make Your Wireless Router More Secure

Routers can be hard-wired or wireless. Wired connections are generally more secure than wireless connections. Many wireless routers come with no security features automatically activated; the default setting often leaves your computer defenseless.

Tip: Activate the Highest Security Settings for Your Wireless Network and Have a Secure Passphrase

These are probably the most protective steps you can take. If you have a wireless network, activate the highest security settings at every access point. There are several security standards. WPA security is more protective than WEP security and WPA2 is more protective than WPA in encrypting data.

Also set up a *passphrase* (also sometimes called a *shared secret*) for access to the network. A passphrase can be from 8 to 63 characters. Longer, random passphrases are more protective (to get a 63-character random passphrase, go to www.grc.com/passwords). You just need to copy and paste this passphrase one time into each computer that's part of the network. You don't manually type it in each time you access the network.

To use WPA2 on Windows XP systems, (1) make sure your computer's built-in network adapter supports WPA2, (2) install the WPA2 update (go to www.microsoft.com and search for *KB893357*), (3) update the drivers on your wireless card and (4) get any needed WPA2 software updates for your router.

Tip: Use MAC Address Filtering

A router with built-in MAC address filtering can help restrict access by letting you specify and restrict the list of computers approved to be on your network. Make sure your computer is on the list so you don't get locked out. To some degree MAC address filtering can help prevent neighbors and strangers from *piggybacking* (using your network). Be aware, however, that a hacker with *sniffer* software can discover authorized MAC addresses (that's why you want to take the more protective steps of activating the highest security settings and using a secure passphrase).

Restrict Wireless Network Signal Strength

The stronger your wireless signal, the greater the likelihood that outsiders can tap into it.

Tip: Don't Overbroadcast Your Signal

Adjust the signal strength so it's just enough to reach each access point and no more. Locate access points in central locations away from windows and outside walls.

Disable Your Unused Wireless Features

Your router or your computer may have a wireless capability.

Tip: Don't Accidentally Broadcast Wirelessly

If you're not using this function (e.g., you use hard-wired Ethernet cables to connect up computers), disable the wireless features so you don't accidentally start broadcasting wirelessly.

Change Your Wireless Network Name and Make It Invisible

Since hackers are aware of the default *SSID*s (public network names) of wireless networks and routers, by default, usually broadcast the public network name, you should do three things. First, change the network name. Second, disable broadcasting the name by turning off or changing the setting to invisible so your router is kept in more of a *stealth mode*. Third, you can go a step further and change the router's IP (Internet Protocol) address setting to make it more difficult to find your router.

Encryption

You may be at the point where you're saying you've read enough about security! It's a personal decision as to how many precautions you decide to take. *Encryption* may be very important if you deal with highly sensitive or confidential information.

Consider Data Encryption for Additional Security

Data encryption programs are designed to keep your information unintelligible unless someone has a code key to unlock the code. These programs can keep outsiders from reading your files but they often can slow down performance, too. You may decide to use either the data encryption features that come with your operating system or third-party encryption programs such as the following to better protect the contents of your computer.

Product Tips: Data Encryption

PGP Desktop Home is designed to be an easy-to-use desktop security solution that protects confidential communications and digitally stored information with strong, broadly accepted, encryption technology. It was created for individuals who want to secure private email, selected files and AOL Instant Messenger (AIM) traffic. It can be used by both casual and power users. *PGP Desktop Professional* includes all of the functionality of PGP Desktop Home plus PGP Whole Disk Encryption for Windows XP users. PGP Whole Disk Encryption provides data encryption for an entire hard disk drive including the operating system, software applications and user data. PGP Corporation, 650/319-9000 [CA] or www.pgp.com

Steganos Security Suite not only encrypts data, it also hides files and drives from outsiders. Steganos GmbH, www.steganos.com

Windows Vista is expected to include encryption capability. You may want to wait a little while before using this feature to make sure any bugs have been corrected so you're not locked out of your computer.

Encrypt Your Email and Signature, If Necessary

Most email isn't encrypted. There are encryption programs with varying levels of security and methods to encrypt emails.

The *electronic* or *digital signature* can be another valuable security tool. It helps to tell the recipient who *signed* the document and that nothing was changed. The electronic signature is a typical feature of encryption programs. However, be aware that nothing is foolproof; electronic signature encryption has been cracked by hackers from time to time.

Lowering Your Risks Off the Internet

Off the Internet, there are a few steps we suggest. Perhaps the single best step you can take is getting a good cross-cut shredder that cuts paper and credit cards into small strips. Cross-cut strips give you more privacy than straight-cut ones. But don't stop there.

Get copies of your credit reports several times a year and check them over for unauthorized activity. Since there are three main credit reporting agencies (Equifax, Experian and TransUnion) and you are entitled to one free credit report from each of them each year (www.annualcreditreport.com), you could save money by just ordering one free report every four months on a rotating basis among the three reporting agencies. However, on such major issues as verifying your *credit standing* and potentially avoiding *identity theft*, it probably is wiser to order from all three agencies more than once a year at the same time (getting one set free and paying for the other sets) to compare the reports.

For additional protection, you could go a step further every quarter and put a no-cost 90-day fraud alert with the credit reporting agencies so you'll need to be contacted before new credit activity (such as new credit cards) can be authorized. There are also fee-based credit reporting services that will alert you if there is a change in your credit status.

It's not enough to lower your profile. You also need to make sure your computer has strong protective software on it. That's what the next chapter is about.

3

Arming Your Computer

When it comes to the Internet, it's dirty dancing. There are bad guys out there trying to get you and you can't just sit back and take it. You have to put up a strong defense.

In the last chapter you saw how a router with a hardware firewall as well as other tips can help give you anonymity on the Internet. But it's not enough to try to hide—you have to arm your computer to prevent attacks and counteract them if they get through your defenses.

Software Firewall

As you read in Chapter 2, a router can give you hardware firewall protection. For essential malware protection, also get a software firewall.

Use One Software Firewall at a Time

A *software firewall* can help control what goes in and comes out of your computer. How many software firewalls are enough? One. With more than one software firewall program turned on at one time, the programs may conflict with one another.

Which software firewall program should you use? Even if your operating system (e.g., Windows) comes with a software firewall, we'd suggest that you get and primarily use a more robust, specialized software firewall program instead.

Product Tip: Software Firewall

ZoneAlarm is a top-rated software firewall program. Zone Labs, Inc., www.zonelabs.com

Tip: Always Have Some Firewall On

If you download a software firewall over the Internet (such as ZoneAlarm) to take over the firewall chores from the one in your operating system, be sure to have your operating system's firewall program turned on during the time you download the more robust software firewall so your computer is not left unprotected. Also, when you turn on your computer, keep your modem cord unplugged from your computer until you look to see and verify that your software firewall loaded up (the firewall program icon should be by the clock on your screen).

Once your software firewall program is installed, it will probably pop up a message on the screen asking your permission before allowing each application (software program) to access the Internet. You should only have to give permanent permission just once for a program you want to use repeatedly.

Warning on Allowing Programs Access to the Net

If you don't recognize the name of a program asking permission to access the Internet, don't answer immediately. Instead, type in the program name in Google (www.google.com) to see if you can determine whether it is a legitimate program. If you're in doubt, just say no.

Don't Be So Quick To Turn Off Your Software Firewall for Tech Support

There may be times when your computer isn't running quite right and a technical support person for one of your software programs will tell you that the problem must be a conflict between the software program and your software firewall. You may then be encouraged to turn off your software firewall to do some troubleshooting, which can extend over quite a period of time.

Be wary of turning off your software firewall while you're connected to the Internet. In many cases, it's something else that's causing the problem, not a firewall conflict. If you do turn off your firewall, you may be making your computer a sitting duck for attacks by hackers. Five years ago, it was estimated that it took 15 minutes for an unprotected computer to become infected; now, some say it takes only 15 seconds.

Tip: Use the Operating System Firewall If Necessary

If you decide to do some tech support testing and turn off a software firewall program that isn't part of your operating system, then at least reactivate the firewall that came with your operating system so you have something in place to protect your computer during the troubleshooting process.

Software Updates

In some ways, your computer defenses come with an expiration date. If hackers discover flaws in your software (such as firewall or antivirus software) and you don't have up-to-date versions, it may just be a matter of time until malware infects your computer. Instead, get software updates so your protection isn't compromised over time.

Update Your Computer's Operating System

The operating system that came with your computer needs *security updates* from time to time to help keep you protected. Get the latest updates to your computer's operating system by going to the software company's site to download fixes and security updates.

Tip: Download More Than Once if Necessary

You may need to go back to the site more than once in one session and run additional checks because sometimes all the updates and fixes are not downloaded to your computer at one time. Keep checking until you are told on the screen that your computer is completely up to date.

Tip: Operating System Automatic Updates May Not Be As Automatic As You Think

Generally, to keep your computer as secure and current as possible (and with the least effort), you may want to enable *automatic updates* from the software manufacturer. However, due to the large number of computers that get automatic updates, it may take many days before your machine is updated. Another concern is that if your machine has been turned off when an update tried to download, your machine may not get updated right away when you turn it back on. So even if automatic updates are turned on, go to the software website every two weeks to manually check for and download updates.

Update Your Internet Browser

Whichever browser you're using, check regularly to make sure you have the latest updates on your computer to minimize security breaches.

Update Your Application Software

Your other software programs (e.g., word processing, spreadsheet, presentation, media player, antivirus, email and instant messaging software) may have security flaws, too, from time to time. So also go to the websites of the providers of your main software applications periodically to check for security updates.

Weekly Disaster-Prevention Program

If you really want your computer to stay protected, you need to follow this seven-step protection routine every week:

#1: Use antivirus, antispyware, antispam and pop-up blocker programs or possibly a security suite.

Besides your hardware and software firewalls, you'll also want to have *one* antivirus program, *one* antispam program, *one* pop-up blocker and *several* antispyware programs.

You need to decide whether you are going to buy separate programs from different companies where a product may be optimized to deal with a particular issue (e.g., antivirus) or one security suite program that contains all or most of the components you want. (You'll still want additional antispyware programs rather than just relying on the one that comes with a security suite.) Security suites differ as to the types of programs they contain.

> **Product Tip: Security Suite**
>
> If you decide to go the security suite route, look at the *ZoneAlarm Internet Security Suite*, which contains a software firewall, an antivirus program, an antispam module, an antispyware program and spim protection. (*Spim* is IM spam.) Zone Labs, Inc., www.zonelabs.com
>
> Note: To see PDFs on the Web while using ZoneAlarm Internet Security Suite, (1) click on the *Privacy* tab, (2) click on the *Main* tab and (3) select *Off* under *Mobile Control*.

Online computer health services offer in one place firewall, antivirus and antispyware automatic online updates and possibly backup and PC maintenance software as well.

#2: Install and activate one antivirus software program.

Having an antivirus program on a computer doesn't necessarily mean that it has been activated to protect you. Make sure the program is active and then go to the software manufacturer's website to get updates ideally daily, but at least weekly. Better yet, once your antivirus program is up to date, enable automatic updates from the software manufacturer.

Tip: Just One Antivirus Program is Enough
Use only one antivirus program. With more than one, the software programs may conflict with one another.

We're going to get a little more techy here. Since viruses can lurk in many places including incoming and outgoing email and instant message attachments, get all the protection you can. When you do an antivirus scan, run a full system scan to scan all files, not just certain types of files. Scan for every type of problem file rather than restricting the options.

Tip: Quick Scanning Habit
Scan *every* file you download, even files from friends.

#3: Run your antivirus program every week in safe mode.

To get the maximum searching and deletion power with an antivirus program, run a full system scan at least every week in *safe mode* because malware can sometimes hide from antivirus programs when you don't do a scan this way.

Safe mode is a special way of booting up (starting or restarting) your computer that minimizes which programs (including malware) are loaded up. To get into safe mode in Windows XP, turn on or restart your computer and tap the *F8 key* every few seconds until the screen (at the top) tells you where to click to get into safe mode. Then follow the screen instructions (or better yet, get someone who's familiar with safe mode to walk you through it the first time). Once you're in safe mode, then run your antivirus program.

#4: Install several antispyware programs, which you should run at least once a week.

Although running only one software firewall program and one antivirus program is recommended, it is a different story with antispyware.

Tip: Run More Than One Antispyware Program

No one antispyware program is going to catch everything. Having and running two to four antispyware programs is probably the optimum number. Update these programs regularly, too, by checking for and downloading any new updates.

Product Tips: Antispyware Programs

Since no one antispyware program catches everything, here are several to consider:

AdAware offers free and fee versions. LavaSoft, Inc., www.lavasoftusa.com

PestPatrol, Computer Associates International, Inc., www.my-etrust.com

Spybot Search and Destroy offers immunization against known threats; removal of spyware infections; and real-time protection to prevent changes to your computer's settings. This popular, free program asks for voluntary donations. Spybot, www.spybot.info

Spy Sweeper can block attempted spyware installations before they can infect your computer with its always-on presence; remove existing spyware infections; and help prevent changes to your computer's settings. Webroot Software, Inc., 866/612-4227 [CO] or www.webroot.com

Spyware Doctor provides three-way spyware protection for your PC through real-time threat blocking, advanced system scanning and immunization against known browser infections. PC Tools, www.pctools.com

After you run an antispyware program, you may need to restart your computer to delete some spyware threats. Some programs automatically restart the system if it's necessary, others remind you to do so and some antispyware programs don't mention restarting at all.

#5: Run your antispyware programs in safe mode.

Just as it is more protective to run your antivirus programs in safe mode, the same is true for running antispyware.

Tip: Run It Again, Sam

After a program finds spyware and cleans it up, run the antispyware program again until it says your computer is clean.

Why? The spyware may *still* be there for two reasons. First, spyware sometimes reinstalls itself and you need to remove it again.

Second, the spyware may still be on your computer if your computer is set to automatically create a *system restore* (see More Disaster Prevention/Recovery Strategies below). The problem may be that your current system has been cleaned by the antispyware but one or more of the older restorable versions is still infected.

Keep going back in time to try to find a clean computer date. If that doesn't work, you may need to turn off system restore and run the antispyware program again.

Tip: Use Real-Time Spyware Monitoring

If an antispyware program allows real-time monitoring (blocking threats as they happen rather than just trying to clean them up later), turn this feature on so your computer can help prevent attacks as they occur and not just clean up after the fact.

Site Tip: Antispyware Site

Spyware Warrior is a website with tips and articles on how to fight spyware and adware; a forum to discuss spyware issues and solutions; and a source for the latest developments. Spyware Warrior, www.spywarewarrior.com

#6: Activate your antispam program.

Antispam programs take different approaches to stopping spam. Some put suspicious email in a separate folder, some only allow approved email addresses to send you email (*whitelisting*) and some use a *challenge/response system* to see whether the sender is a person or a spamming computer. The right one for you is a matter of personal preference.

Product Tips: Antispam Programs

Cloudmark Desktop is designed to block spam and phishing attacks. Cloudmark, 415/543-1220 [CA] or www.cloudmark.com

iHateSpam for Outlook is a spam filter that can dramatically reduce the junk email you find in your mailbox. Sunbelt Software, www.sunbelt-software.com

MailFrontier Desktop is designed to start working immediately to block and remove junk email such as spam and phish from your inbox. There are no rules you need to create, no lists to populate, nothing — the program does it for you. As you use MailFrontier Desktop, it continues to learn about the email you don't like to provide better protection for your inbox. You can change the aggressiveness of the spam detection settings, update your own allowed/block lists, use a challenge/response system and even block all email in a specific language. MailFrontier, Inc., www.mailfrontier.com

Mailshell provides ways to control spam. Mailshell.com, Inc., www.mailshell.com

#7: Back up your clean computer.

Once you run your antivirus and antispyware programs and your computer is free of viruses, worms, Trojan horses, spyware and other detectable threats, back up your "clean" computer or at least any new files from the last time you cleaned your computer files and backed them up.

Tip: Get Clean for a System Restore

This is also a good time to make sure the *system restore*

feature in your operating system is turned on so you have a *clean date* to go back to if you need to restore your computer's system. If system restore has been turned on, it allows you to put your computer's programs back into the state and shape they were in on a prior date. As a reminder of your clean system date, send yourself an email with the subject line "Clean computer date" so you'll know later on when your computer was cleaned up and safe should you need to pick a restore date. (See Chapter 13 for how to back up your computer.)

More Disaster Prevention/Recovery Strategies

If disaster strikes, you may want to go back in time to undo the damage but life doesn't work that way. Or does it? Read on.

Be Prepared to Go Back in Time

As we've seen there may come a time where you need to use the system restore function that is part of your computer's operating system. A more complete solution is using a *rollback software* program that lets you go back in time to undo more of the harm done to your computer.

Product Tips: Rollback Programs

A rollback software program such as *Norton GoBack* (Symantec, www.symantec.com) or the top-rated *Retro-spect* (EMC Corp., www.dantz.com) lets you go back in time to undo the mischief done to your machine and re-store earlier settings.

Prepare a Current Emergency Recovery Disk

Disaster can strike your computer at any time. Have on hand a disk with the latest version of your operating system, your backup soft-ware and the drivers for the hardware on (or attached to) your com-puter. Use your antivirus program's emergency disk preparation feature (or possibly your operating system's) to create the disk.

Reinstall Your Operating System, If Necessary

In some cases, viruses and other intruders are just too crafty to catch and totally remove. The only cure may be to reinstall your operating system and wipe out all the programs and data on your disk. A reinstallation should get rid of virtually all viruses or spyware that have been too persistent to remove any other way. Hopefully, you'll have a good, clean, current backup already on hand.

Run Only the Software You Need

You may have software programs that load every time you start your computer but that you never use.

Tip: Turn Off Unneeded Programs

Turn off (disable) communication programs (e.g., an instant messenger) that may be on your computer, but not used, which can open up *ports* (access points to your computer).

Look for Danger Signals Daily

On the bottom of your computer screen by the clock, you should see icons for your firewall and antivirus and antispyware programs that are always on. Take a look at the icons at least twice a day to see whether any of them are flashing a warning signal to you that something is amiss.

Be a Tech Plumber and Look for Leaks

There are tools to discover leaks and available ports to enter your computer's system.

Product Tips: Tools to Find Hacker Entry Points

LeakTest is a free testing program to determine whether your firewall is working. Gibson Research Corp., www.grc.com

ShieldsUP! is a quick, popular, free Internet security checkup and information service. Gibson Research Corp., www.grc.com

Don't Be the Source for an Attack on Your Own Network

Although companies spend a lot to prevent computer attacks from the outside, many of the attacks come accidentally from insiders.

Sometimes computer networks get infected when individuals (a) log on remotely from hot spots with poor security or (b) inadvertently sync up using infected computers (those that haven't had their weekly disaster-prevention steps done on a regular basis).

Tighten Up Macro Security in Your Everyday Software Applications

A *macro* is one computer instruction that carries out a series of computer instructions. Some viruses hide in macros in computer files.

How to Tighten Macro Security

If you're using Microsoft Word, for example, here are the steps: (1) click *Tools,* (2) click *Options,* (3) click the *Security* tab, (4) click the *Macro Security* button and (5) click the *level of security* you want.

The steps for doing Microsoft Office commands will change in the next version of Office because options known as *Ribbons* are generally replacing toolbars, drop-down menus and dialog boxes.

See All Your Files, File Extensions and Folders

Some viruses and other malware like to hide from your view in hidden files and folders. Although you can change the usual view of files and folders to also see what's hidden, some people find seeing this all-encompassing view too distracting. However, if you want to see what's hidden, in Windows Explorer, (1) click *Tools*; (2) click *Folder Options*; (3) click *View*; (4) check *Show Hidden files and folders*; (5) uncheck *Hide file extensions for known file types*; and (6) uncheck *Hide protected operating system files.*

Have a Fast Enough Computer

This may be the most overlooked item on anyone's security checklist. To keep your computer protected, you need to regularly use antivirus and antispyware programs to check and safeguard your computer's contents. Since running these programs is very intensive work for your computer and can take time, you don't want a computer that is so slow it discourages you from running these safety checks.

Use Virtualization to Run Virtual Machines

If you're really adventuresome and have a techy gene or two, you might venture into the realm of running virtual machines. With virtual machine software, you create a virtual (nonphysical) clone of your computer to venture out into the Internet. The original is safe and sound at home. If the clone gets infected out on the Internet, your main system is unaffected. You just get rid of the infected clone, create another copy and send in the clones. If you're curious and also capable of handling this form of virtual reality, take a look at the *Spyware Weekly Newsletter* at http://spywareinfo.com/articles/vmware/baintro.php

It's a good feeling to know that you've taken steps to better protect your computer. Now you're ready to handle your email and Web searching with more protection in place.

Part 2

Making Small Talk and Big Talk

Controlling Communication Overload

4

Controlling Email and Spam

It seems people don't cross a room anymore to ask someone to dance. Instead, they text or email a message and wait for a response. No response can mean "No, thank you." What's next may be an emailed marriage proposal, which doubles the risk of rejection because a proposal has to get past a spam filter first.

Since email is here to stay, you need to find ways to control the barrage (and garbage) of information that is undoubtedly coming your way, set up automatic systems to separate legitimate email from spam and find quicker and better ways to read and respond to email.

Because communication overload is not just from email and communication keeps evolving in its usage, popularity and forms, there are also chapters in Part 2 on instant messaging, text messaging and phone communication. It's interesting to see the communication evolution: emails have supplemented and partly replaced phone calls; text messaging and instant messaging are now doing the same to emails; and voice-text messaging may replace typed text messaging in the near future. Another trend is for email and IM services to be integrated together so it's easy to switch between them.

But email is still very much with us. Let's begin by considering the impact email has on how we work as well as how we think.

Emails and IQ

With the popularity of email, instant and text messaging comes new questions on how and when to use this technology. How often is often enough when it comes to checking email? How many times per day? How many times per hour? And how quickly should a reply be sent? How should instant or text messages be handled? Before you answer these questions, read on.

Email/Text Message Study

A study by a King's College, London University psychiatrist of over 1,000 participants found that their intelligence declined as tasks were interrupted by incoming emails and text messages.

The Study Results

Users suffered a 10% drop in IQ scores. The deterioration in mental capacity was the direct result of an addiction to technology. With such an addiction, people responded to every email immediately or within 10 minutes and were "happy" to interrupt a business or social meeting to respond to an email or text message.

Email addicts were bombarded by context switches and developed an inability to distinguish between trivial and significant messages.

Controlling Email by Reducing It

If you're like most of us, you have a love-hate relationship with your email. Billions of email messages are sent *every day* in the U.S. It only *seems* like you're getting all of them. On average, people are spending about one-third more time on email than they did just one or two years ago.

If you're like most people, emails exert great time pressure. Email messages take up time when you receive them, save them or delete them. They also convey a false sense of urgency simply due to the instantaneous nature of the medium (including the possibility that the sender may know that messages have been read).

And emails often add an additional layer of communication. Some people will send an email and then send a voicemail message telling you they've sent an email message.

You need to find ways to better control email and there are three keys to doing so: (1) reduce the quantity that comes in, (2) reduce how much time is spent on received email and (3) reduce the quantity that goes out.

Reduce How Much Email Comes In

If you start by reducing how much email comes in, you'll have a better shot at reducing the time you spend on email including the messages you send.

Don't Advertise Your Email Address to Everyone

Very simply, don't give out your email address to everyone. Have two business cards — one with and one without your email address — and give out the email one selectively. Don't pick an obvious email address such as Mary@mycompany.com. For less essential email, consider getting a free email address that can be abandoned if spam overwhelms it.

Product Tips: Free Email Addresses

Google Gmail offers a large storage capacity. Google, Inc., www.google.com

Hotmail offers free email addresses that can give you the freedom to drop an address that becomes a target of spam. Microsoft Corp., www.hotmail.com

Windows Live Mail, in a beta version at the time this book is being written, will replace Hotmail. It is designed to improve how you receive, send and organize messages. Microsoft Corp., http://ideas.live.com

Warning: Access to Online Emails

Read the fine print before you sign up for online storage arrangements. For example, at the time this book is being written, all Yahoo! accounts (including Yahoo! Mail) have a *No Right of Survivorship and Non-Transferability* clause in the standard terms and conditions where your death ends access by anyone (even a spouse/executor wanting access to your personal or business emails) to information stored online.

Have a Rules-Based Email Program

If you get a lot of email, you'll need a good *rules-based* email software program to manage your email. A rules-based program can be a real timesaver in two ways:

First, a rules-based program uses *filters* — criteria you specify to screen your email. It's like giving instructions to a bouncer at your email front door to know who to keep out and where to direct those who are permitted in. The filters in a rules-based program specify accepting or blocking messages from certain people or on certain topics.

Second, a rules-based program helps you better prioritize your messages. Filters can alert you to emails marked "urgent" as well as those from key individuals, such as your boss, and can literally sound an alarm.

Tip: Filters Can Highlight Priority Emails

Filters can highlight important emails you want to read ASAP by sending them to a special high-priority folder so you can deal with your most important emails in a timely manner.

Tip: Rules Can Keep Your Emails Organized

The rules feature can also help you organize and file emails by automatically archiving messages older than a certain designated date or filing messages by subject into separate folders.

Product Tip: Rules-Based Email Program
Eudora is an alternative email program that has received
rave reviews for quite some time. Qualcomm, Inc.,
800/238-3672 [CA] or www.eudora.com

Avoid Giving an Email Address

If a site really doesn't need your email address, see if you can avoid
giving any email address.

Look for Opt-Out Boxes to Check

When you sign up for services at some websites, see if you can reduce
your exposure to spam, spyware and unnecessary emails by
unchecking the boxes for (a) receiving email offers and other solicita-
tions and (b) letting the website remember your email address in the
future.

Read the Privacy Policy

Although almost no one actually reads those privacy policies, you
might be surprised to learn what you're agreeing to as far as the site's
use of your email address and your personal information if you click
the OK button.

Try "Eom" to Reduce Unnecessary Reply Emails

Many times you may send an email and there is no real need for
someone to respond or even say thank you. If indicating *FYI* (for your
information) still causes unnecessary responses, try putting *eom* (end
of *m*essage) in the subject line of your email (or even in a cellphone or
mobile device IM or text message you send). Since not everyone
knows what this means, make sure the recipient is educated about
this timesaver or you'll get another email or message asking you to
explain "eom."

Stop Unfounded Forwards

One way spammers pick up email addresses is by seeing forwarded
emails that contain the email addresses of five to ten prior forwards
of a well-intentioned but often groundless forwarded message. First,
go to *www.snopes.com* to check out hoaxes and urban legends to avoid
forwarding them on to others. Then if a message is truly legitimate

and important, copy and paste the message (without all the prior addresses) into a new email.

Five Ways to Put a Bite into Spam

In many cases, more than 75 percent of email is spam. Every spam (junk) email that's blocked means more time for you to read your real email and actually get work done. Blocking spam also lessens the chance of your computer picking up spyware or a virus from the spam and your needing to spend time cleaning up an infected computer.

1. Use a *spam filter* or antispam program.

Your ISP (Internet Service Provider) may catch spam with its own filter before it hits your email in-box. Some ISPs delete spam while others separate it from your other email so you can check whether it's really spam. Your email program may have antispam capabilities that include having the sender to take an additional step (such as a *computational proof* where the sender must make a computation specific to the message or the receiver) the first time a message is sent to you by that person. Or you may decide to get an antispam program that filters your email by looking at not only the email's subject line but also its content.

Tip: Challenge/Response Email System

Another approach is to purchase an antispam program that uses a challenge/response email system. When you receive an email from someone not already in your email address book, your computer sends a challenge question or task (e.g., copying randomly-generated numbers on a screen) to prove that it's a person and not an automatically generated (spam) email. Unless the challenge is met, the email does not go through.

Tip: Whitelisting Email System

Another alternative is to go with a whitelisting program that only allows email from senders you specify in advance.

Product Tips: Antispam Programs

See Chapter 3 for information on *Cloudmark Desktop*, *iHateSpam*, *MailFrontier Desktop* and *Mailshell*.

2. Avoid accidentally replying to spammers.

Find out if your email program is responding to spammers without your knowledge.

Warning on Default Email Program Responses

With some email programs, the default setting is to always send a response, even to spam. This verifies the validity of your email address for spammers and lets them send more spam to you. Check the automatic response setting on your email program.

3. Don't answer spam or respond to the "remove me" option.

Tip: Silence is a Better Response Sometimes

If you respond to spam by requesting to have your email address taken off a list, you've just confirmed to the spammer that yours is a valid email address.

4. Keep your main email address off the Net.

Warning on Spammers

Spammers scan the Internet looking for email addresses in places such as chat rooms, newsgroups and online guest books. This is where a disposable, free email address can come in handy.

5. Be careful with emails with no subject line or just "Hi" in the subject line.

This tip is so important it's also in Chapter 2, which covers lowering your online presence. Avoid opening emails that have no subject line or one that's too friendly or generic such as "Hi" or "Hello There." This is often a spam email that may inadvertently come from a friend's computer that has been infected with a virus. If you get an email with a suspicious or nonexistent subject line, call or email first (without hitting "reply") to confirm its validity before opening up the email.

Reduce How Much Time You Spend On Email

Here are 11 ways to better manage your email time:

1. Limit the number of mailboxes.

If you have fewer places to check for email during the day (or night), that'll reduce your email processing time. Some email programs let you check multiple email accounts at the same time.

Tip: Use Just the Essential Email Addresses

If possible, use just one email address for work and another for personal email. (You might also have a public email for posting to newsgroups or in chatrooms.)

2. Switch to unified messaging.

One way to get communications under control may be cutting down all the places you have to check for your messages. That's where *unified messaging* comes in. All of your voice mail, email, text messages, instant messages and faxes can be placed in one unified messaging mailbox.

How It Works

With this universal in-box, you can either listen and reply to your voice mail, email, text and instant messages and faxes from a phone or use your computer or mobile device and Internet access.

Unified messaging may be offered now (or soon) by your email or instant messenger provider, your ISP (Internet Service Provider), your telephone company or other third-party providers. The trend will be for companies to offer you a package of services including email, instant and text messaging, phone service, Internet access and TV along with unified messaging.

Product Tips: Unified Messaging Software

Office Communicator 2005 is designed to: (a) manage in a single view instant messages, email, voice and other business communications and (b) allow switching from instant messaging to a video chat or conference call with the click of a button. At the time of the writing of this book, it is being beta-tested. Microsoft Corp., www.microsoft.com

Onebox is for fax, email, voice and conferencing services. J2 Global Communications, www.onebox.com

Windows Live together with *Windows Live Messenger* (the next generation MSN Messenger) are designed to let you manage in one site over the Internet email, real-time text, video and voice communications, calendars, tasks, contacts, photos, podcasts, RSS feeds (including images) and blogs. They are in beta testing at the time this book is being written. Microsoft Corp., http://ideas.live.com

3. Check email at set times, not constantly.

It's better to use set blocks of time or appointments with yourself, if possible, throughout the day to reduce the number of daily interruptions. (That's why you may not want to get a mouse with an LED that lights up as each email or IM comes in!)

And if the results of that King's College study on emails and IQs are correct, you'll also be sharper and better able to separate the important from the unimportant.

You will also be training coworkers and other recipients not to expect an immediate response every time. If you respond immediately to every email, you'll find your email load and stress level increase even more.

4. Set up a clearly-defined message priority system.

When you use priority terms for your messages such as "Urgent," "Regular" or "Special Attention," make sure you and your email correspondents have determined in advance what these terms mean. Another option is to include a deadline date or response-needed date.

5. Scan emails efficiently.

Don't read every email. Instead, first scan subject lines, message headers and sender names (or set up a filter to do this) to separate the wheat from the chaff.

6. Prioritize your emails and email time.

Prioritize and respond to your most important *and* urgent messages. Then go to those important but not urgent messages. See how many of them you can reply to or delegate quickly.

7. Know how to handle email attachments.

There are three big issues with attachments, the files attached to or sent with emails.

First, opening attached files is the main way viruses and worms are spread. Computer *malware* (see Chapter 1) takes advantage of your trusting a known source, such as the known sender of an attached file. So, open every attachment, even one from a known sender, only *after* scanning it for viruses and other malware.

Second, postpone opening messages with attachments, unless they're from a key person because doing so can be very time consuming. Whenever possible, handle email attachments together by scanning for malware and then opening them during one block of time.

Third, be diligent about clearing out attachments you've received so you don't run out of room for other email you'll be receiving!

8. Delete or file daily.

Take time every day to delete as many messages as possible or to file them in an appropriate folder. It's easier to deal with emails while they're fresh so you don't have to go back and reread them to make decisions.

A good time for email pruning and filing is while you're on hold during phone calls.

9. Create an email message management system.

Your email program may come with several generic folders and also let you create your own. Use electronic folders for storing and organizing messages. Ideally, set up message rules so files are automatically put into the correct folder.

Tip: Use Email Calendar Reminders

Your email program may let you calendar reminders to take action on emails or alert you when emails arrive from certain people.

Tip: Finding Emails Quickly

If you need to find an email, the email software's search feature may be good enough or you could use a desktop search program. Desktop search programs work differently as far as what they search (e.g., some search emails, attachments, instant messages and files at the same time). See Chapter 11 for more information on desktop search programs. In general, it's best to have well-organized email folders and use a search program as a supplement, but not as a substitute, for good organization.

10. Archive important but inactive messages.

Archive email you need to store but don't need to have right on hand. Your email program may have an automatic archiving feature.

Warning on Archiving Email

Archiving email has become more of a legal concern so companies are getting legal advice on what to keep and for how long.

11. Learn the organizing features in your email software.

One of these days, take an hour to discover the shortcuts that are built into your email program. Shortcuts could save you time every day.

For example, your email program may let you color code email messages, where you might use say, "red" for urgent, "yellow" for moderate urgency and "green" for information only.

Reduce the Quantity of Outgoing Email

Here are four ways to reduce outbound email:

1. Determine if email is the best way to communicate.

There are times you might want to avoid email. A telephone call or instant message may be faster and/or more suitable.

Warning on When *Not* to Use Email

Email can be too impersonal, removing the human connection so important for work teams and relationships in general. It doesn't allow for the give-and-take that a telephone call or a face-to-face meeting can give you to facilitate communication. Don't use email as a way to avoid face-to-face dealings with others.

2. Limit distribution lists.

Don't send someone an email unless they really need to see it. Maybe they'll do the same favor for you someday.

3. Don't advertise email addresses unnecessarily.

If you forward an email, don't include the email addresses of all the other recipients of the email, unless necessary.

Tip: Use Bccs When Appropriate

To prevent your email address from becoming part of a circulated list, encourage others to use the *bcc* (blind carbon copy) function. This allows the sender to send out an email to many people but it hides the email addresses of the recipients. This helps prevent those addresses from being harvested by spammers. (See Chapter 2 for more information on bcc.)

4. Use intranets or wikis when available.

If you work for a large organization, post announcements on a central-access area on an intranet or create your own workgroup-specific website rather than just using email for everything.

More companies are using a *wiki*—a giant online bulletin board that's part of a company site where thoughts, ideas and company news items are posted instead of being emailed to everyone.

Email Security—Encryption

Encryption may not only protect the contents of your messages but also your email address(es). Powerful encryption can help ensure that only your intended receiver can decipher your message. An encryption program is ideal for anyone with proprietary or sensitive data.

Product Tips: Encryption Software

HushMail is a Web-based encrypted email service designed to let you encrypt messages and store and share files from almost any Web-capable PC. Hush Communications Corp., www.hushmail.com

PGP Desktop Home, as more fully described in Chapter 2, is a desktop security solution that uses encryption technology. PGP Corporation, 650/319-9000 [CA] or www.pgp.com

Changing Your Email Service

Even if you have your email under control, you may be unhappy with your email service provider or want to switch to one that is less likely to be a target for hackers. (As with Internet browsers, more widespread usage usually means a more attractive target to hackers.)

Chances are you're reluctant to change your email service because you don't want to lose your existing emails. Fortunately, there are products out that may help you more easily make the switch to a new email service.

Product Tip: Email Converter

Aid4Mail helps you convert your old emails if you switch to another email service. The program supports many (but not all) popular email client programs. Fookes Software, www.aid4mail.com

Product Tip: Email Forwarding

TrueSwitch helps you switch email accounts or ISPs by copying your personal data (e.g., address book, calendar, stored emails, favorites, etc.) to your new account; providing people in your address book with your new email address; and forwarding emails from your old email/ISP account to your new one (as long as the old account is kept open and the password isn't changed). Esaya, Inc., www.trueswitch.com

Features to Consider Before Making a Switch

Before signing up, check out the following:

Speed and Reliability

You can't afford to have your email down and unavailable. The major computer magazines (*PC Magazine* and *PC World*) do surveys each year on customer satisfaction levels.

Accessibility

If you travel a lot, find out the connection options (and costs) to access your email.

Tip: Have a Back Up Plan

Remember that even if you have a high-speed (e.g., DSL or cable-modem) connection, it may also pay to have dial-up capability as a backup in case your high-speed connection goes down. More computer manufacturers are offering another alternative—a built-in EV-DO, *3G* (third generation) wireless broadband card for Internet connections on nationwide wireless networks. This card picks up a wireless radio signal from the air much like your cellphone. *HSDPA* and *EDGE* are two other 3G wireless card technologies.

Mobile Accessibility

If you're going to access your email from your cellphone or other mobile device, see whether you'll be able to avoid endless clicking through multiple menus and instead just click once or twice to read your email. It's also nice to have email automatically pushed to your screen so you're immediately notified of its arrival.

See whether you'll be able to view attachments. Also check out how email is synchronized with your computer-based account. See whether messages read on your mobile device show up as having been read when you log on to your email account from your computer. Also see whether they're kept on the server as a permanent record.

Product Tips: Access to Email and Documents While on the Go

mail2web.com provides a free web-based email retrieval application that allows users from anywhere to anonymously pick up their email from almost any POP3 and IMAP4 email server. No registration is required to access or use the application. To retrieve or send email with mail2web.com, just enter your email address and password. You can easily read, reply, forward and even delete messages while you're away from your regular email program. SoftCom Technology Consulting, Inc., www.mail2web.com

MT1 lets you listen to your emails and Word documents while on the go using your computer, cellphone, Pocket PC or iPod/MP3 player. MagneticTime, www.magnetictime.com

Antispam and Antivirus Filters and Programs
See what the provider offers to save you time and grief.

Restrictions on Downloads and VoIP
Due to bandwidth concerns, some companies are making it more difficult for consumers to use the Internet to send or download video, audio and photo files as well as to make Internet phone calls (VoIP). In some cases, the download transfer speed is reduced, Internet phone calls aren't allowed or a higher rate is charged for phone calls to get priority on a network.

By contrast, other companies are offering access to high-resolution downloads and unlimited online storage space for items such as digital photos.

Maximum Size of Attachments

This is overlooked too often. Find out the maximum size attachments you can send and receive with your email service.

Storage Size Options and Locations

Warning: Enough Storage Space

If your email storage space is too limited, even one incoming email with a large attachment may cause all your other incoming email to be bumped and returned to the senders. Clear out or archive attachments you've received so you don't run out of room or look for an online provider offering enough or unlimited storage space.

If you save email rather than regularly delete it, you need a place to store it—on your email provider's server, your computer's hard disk or on an external backup disk. The trend is towards ISPs (Internet Service Providers) allowing you large or even unlimited online storage space.

Tip: Online Storage Advantages

Online storage gives you the advantage of having access to all of your emails no matter where you are if you have an Internet connection and the provider doesn't go out of business.

Warning on Online Storage

There are three possible disadvantages with online storage: (1) the access speed may be too slow depending on your Internet connection, (2) security issues may be present when your information is stored somewhere other than on your computer or archived storage media and (3) with certain online accounts, when you die, no one may have access to your account and the contents may be destoyed. For example, at the time this book is being written, all Yahoo! accounts (including Yahoo! Mail and Yahoo! Photos) have a *No Right of Survivorship and Non-Transferability* clause in the standard terms and conditions where your death ends access by anyone (even a spouse/executor wanting access to personal or business emails/photos) to information stored online.

Choice of Address
See whether you can have an email address that includes your company's domain name on the Web.

Organizing and Prioritizing Emails
Check if there are good folder and filter systems in place. See if color coding or another method is available to prioritize your emails.

Extra Notifications
See whether your email program can call you or contact your mobile device to let you know an email has come in or can use *push technology* to automatically send an email to your device.

Email is more than controlling spam, reducing the time spent on email and finding the right email service provider. You also want to write email messages that have impact and reflect well on you. Read about email writing tips in Chapter 5.

5

Email Writing Tips

Making a good presentation increases your chances of someone accepting a dance invitation from you. Similarly, knowing how to write and frame an email increases your chances of success off the dance floor.

One Dozen Email Writing Essentials

Most email messages are a cross between a note and a phone conversation. As such, they need to be brief and easy to read. And because it's generally more difficult to read type on a screen (than on paper) and people are inundated with email, you want to make your emails as easy and inviting to read as possible.

1. **Determine the recipient of your message in advance.**

   Decide who really needs the message. Knowing your audience will help you better frame the message.

   Indicate if a message should be restricted. Too many messages are copied and forwarded indiscriminately. You may want to include a confidentiality statement in case your email is mistakenly received by someone else.

2. **Write a subject line that gets noticed and isn't rejected as spam.**

   If your subject line looks too much like a sales pitch, it may be automatically rejected by a spam filter (remember the wedding proposal email on the first page of Chapter 4). Make your subject relevant to the reader and to the content of your message.

3. **Put the most important information right up front including any request for action.**

   If the action item is important, include it up front in the subject line as well as in the email message itself. In the opening paragraph, spell out what's needed, any deadline and why it's important. If, however, your main purpose is reinforcing a relationship, put relationship-building content in the first paragraph(s) and any request for action in a subsequent paragraph.

4. **Pay special attention to tone.**

   Use the appropriate tone, style and emotional content for the intended audience. Avoid jokes and sarcasm. Be careful about conveying negative information through email. Warm up email by using the recipient's name at least once and preferably twice; otherwise, email can be too cold and impersonal. Limit the use of words (except acronyms) or sentences in all upper case letters. Besides being difficult to read, overuse of caps is the online equivalent of screaming at someone.

5. **Be brief.**

   Using block style, write brief, concise messages in short paragraphs (with no more than three sentences each) that put your main points right up front so that they show up on the screen before any scrolling.

6. **Use good graphic design elements.**

   In addition to short paragraphs, use the following elements to make it easier to read your emails:

   • Bullets or numbers to list key ideas without long, wordy sentences

- Subheads to organize main points and guide your reader(s)

- White space to prevent and break up dense text

- Boldface and color for highlighting key points but don't overdo it

- Appropriate graphics that don't take too long to load

- A *sans serif* typefont such as Arial (it's easier to read onscreen); avoid the use of all upper or lower case letters, which are difficult to read

7. Use Net Lingo.

Net lingo in informal emails (as well as in instant and text messages) is a quick, shorthand way of writing that saves time, reduces keystrokes and speeds up communication (assuming you're using commonly understood terms). There are two basic types of Net lingo: abbreviations and acronyms.

Abbreviations are shortened forms of words without a period such as *info* for information and *conf* for conference.

Acronyms are used extensively and are pronounced in two different ways: (1) Letter by letter, e.g., *FAQ* (frequently asked questions) is pronounced "F," "A," "Q" or (2) as a word, e.g., random access memory is written *RAM* and pronounced like the word "ram."

Product Tips: Sites to Learn the Lingo

AOL provides an acronym dictionary at
http://www.aim.com/acronyms.adp?aolp=

Netlingo.com can get you up to speed on computer talk. Netlingo, Inc., www.netlingo.com

8. Read carefully.

This goes for rereading a message you're about to send as well as reading messages you've received. See if your email program has an "Unsend" feature, too—just in case you want to recall something you just sent.

9. **When responding to a message, clearly refer to the original message you received if it's not included in the reply.**

   If it is included, be sure to use one or more greater than signs (>) before copy that the correspondent sent to you, which means "this is what you wrote." (This may be done automatically for you when you highlight text and press "Reply.")

   Include only those parts to which you are responding. You may want to boldface your responses or use a larger font size to make them clearly stand out.

10. **Avoid sending unsolicited or unexpected attachments (files) without first notifying the recipient.**

    If your attachment arrives unexpectedly, your email may be deleted as spam since the "best" way to catch a computer virus, worm or other unwanted visitor is by opening up an infected attachment. Instead first call or send a text (no attachment) email to alert them. If you send a large file and it fills up someone's email in-box so all their other incoming email is rejected, they won't be looking favorably upon you. Find out both the sending and receiving size limitations of attachments.

11. **Know when to use *reply* versus *reply to all*.**

    You don't want to accidentally broadcast a reply that was meant for only one recipient. Make it a habit to click *Reply* and only click *Reply to all* when appropriate. Also see Chapter 2 on bcc's.

12. **Assume email sent from work will be read by your employer.**

    The workplace norm is for companies to have email scanning software to determine whether email uses and content are appropriate.

Although emails are a staple of our daily life, increasingly instant messaging (IM) is gaining in popularity. In Chapter 6, see how IM requires the proper "netiquette."

6

Instant Messaging

Just as you should ask first on the dance floor before cutting in on someone, it's important to knock first when you're instant messaging (IM).

Instant messaging sent from a computer or a mobile device lets you reach out and connect with others. IM is almost a hybrid between a phone call and an email where you communicate in real time by typing rather than talking and each person's messages appear on the screens. You can even have simultaneous, independent IM conversations but multitasking runs the risk of overtasking your brain.

IM is popular for six reasons:

1. It transmits faster than email—it's real-time, instant communication.

2. There are fewer steps to send and receive with IM than with email.

3. Unlike email, you know whether the other person is online unless they're blocking you.

4. IM has the give-and-take feel of an ongoing "conversation" even though it's all in writing. With IM animated *avatars* (small, graphical images), you can even give some nonverbal cues (nodding or shaking heads, smiles).

5. For collaborative work or for customer support, IM can be a great channel of communication with its private group IM chats.

Using IM to Diagnose and Fix Computers Remotely

Windows Live Messenger together with the *Windows Live Safety* scanner will soon be able to help with the remote handling of PC tune-ups, finding and removing malware and diagnosing performance issues on a remote computer. Both products are being beta-tested as this book is being written. Microsoft Corp., www.microsoft.com

6. The IM features list keeps growing and may include telephone calls; audio and video chats; voice mail; conference calling; audio-chat recording; file and photo sharing and transfers; text messaging and other capabilities.

Warning on Cyber Trails

As with email, anything you write leaves at least a cyber trail and can be saved and printed. So exercise caution, good judgment and restraint.

IM and Interruptions

IM is *interrupt driven*. It is analogous to someone knowing that you're at home and barging in unannounced saying "I'm here," asking for some of your time regardless of what you're doing at the moment. It's a virtual barging into your office, cubicle, computer or mobile device.

Netiquette

With more and more devices connected to the Internet all the time, IM can make you all too available. That's why you need to have some ready responses to take control of IM and practice some considerate "netiquette" of your own.

IM Courtesy

When you're initiating an IM, start by asking (as you should do on a phone call) whether the person is available. You could start your message by asking "Busy?" or "Got a minute?" If your buddy doesn't have time to chat, it easily lets them off the hook.

And if you're receiving an IM and you don't have time to chat, let your buddy know that as well. Have short reasons ready: "Sorry, on the phone" or "On a big deadline...later." When you're ready to sign off, a simple "Bye" or "Gotta go" can do the trick.

Controlling Incoming IM

There are ways to control who can send IM and when they can send it.

The Buddy List

Instant messaging lets you set up a special *buddy* or *contact list* that can give you and your IM contacts immediate access to one another. The IM software indicates whether a contact is online and if so, you can then send the contact a message, which pops up on their screen in a little box right in the middle of whatever they're doing.

Make sure you restrict users to just your buddy list. Unless absolutely needed, keep IM simple and disable advanced features, file sharing and file transfer features.

Blocking Out

IM programs also have blocking features to prevent selected (or all) individuals from knowing you're online or sending you messages. You just may want to use this invisibility feature more often than not.

Knock-Knock

Most IM programs let you see a *knock-knock* message from people not on your buddy or contact list. This lets you decide whether to accept the message, block all future messages from that person or just warn them not to send any more.

Instant Message Aggregators and More

The trend is toward consumer IM allowing direct communication
with other instant messaging services (*interoperability*) and for corporate IM messaging systems (e.g., *Lotus Sametime*) working with consumer platforms such as AOL and Apple iChat. Some security experts
say interoperability will bring a new set of security problems.

If you trade instant messages with someone who uses a different IM
service and the two IM services do not have an instant-messaging
sharing pact, you may still need an *instant messaging aggregator* or an
IM program so the two of you can communicate. Whenever you use
IM, see whether encryption and *authentication* (verifying the identity
of your chatting partner) are available.

Product Tips: IM Aggregators and More

Gaim is an instant message aggregator. If you have IM
accounts on several different IM services, you can log in
to multiple accounts on multiple IM networks simultaneously. Gaim, http://gaim.sourceforge.net/about.php

Trillian is a stand-alone IM program that supports AIM,
ICQ, MSN, Yahoo Messenger and IRC. While Trillian can
be thought of as a product that aggregates your instant
messaging world, it does not control or require the existence of any other IM applications to function properly.
Trillian connects on its own to the IM networks it supports and acts independently of other IM software. So,
for example, you don't need AOL Instant Messenger on
your computer for Trillian to successfully connect to the
AIM service. Other features include audio chat, file transfers, group chats, chat rooms, buddy icons, encrypted
messaging (AIM/ICQ), privacy settings and support for
SMS (Short Message Service also called text messaging).
Cerulean Studios, www.ceruleanstudios.com

Security Issues with IM

In general, IM is not a secure way of communicating especially when used wirelessly at hot spots.

Warning: Don't Put Yourself in a Hot Spot

If possible, avoid using a wireless (e.g., Wi-Fi) connection at a hot spot (e.g., a coffee shop) to connect to the Internet. Although some hot spots have better security protection than others, as a first line of defense, try to minimize your use of hot spots, especially if you're dealing with sensitive information and instant messaging. See Chapter 2 for hot spot security suggestions.

Software programs can help keep your instant messages confidential and provide protection against unauthorized IM traffic.

Product Tip: IM Security Program

IMsecure Pro helps secure IM inbound and outbound communications, even across multiple clients. If all parties to an IM conversation are using the program, it is designed to also encrypt all sides of the conversation. Zone Labs, Inc., www.zonelabs.com

Just as with email, there are security issues in clicking on links and opening attachments (see Chapter 2) and you'll want an antivirus program that offers protection against malware such as IM worm attachments. Some of the most "intelligent" malware is found in IM worms. Smarter IM worms can IM chat with you and try to convince you to click on the "safe" link in the IM. When it comes to worms, consider the source.

Spim

And as with email, you can get junk messages, which in IM talk are known as *spim*. At this time, the best defense against spim is to restrict your buddy/contact list and to avoid clicking on hyperlinks in IM messages. Commercial products are starting to protect against spim, too.

Product Tip: Antispim Protection
ZoneAlarm Internet Security Suite offers protection against spim in addition to providing a software firewall, an antivirus program, an antispam module and an antispyware program.
Zone Labs, Inc., www.zonelabs.com

IM and email aren't the only ways to communicate in writing. Text messaging is big, too, and in an emergency it may be a better way of communicating than a phone call. See the next chapter to find out why.

7

Text Messaging

O n the dance floor you worry about having two left feet. Off the
dance floor it's usually a disadvantage to be all thumbs. But
that's not the case with text messaging.

We are big fans of text messaging (also called SMS—Short Message
Service). Text messaging respects the privacy of the recipient and is
less intrusive than instant messaging or phone calls. Unlike IM,
there's a similarity to emails because you are not putting the person
on the spot where they have to tell you "Not now" if they don't want
to communicate with you at that time.

If you do a lot of text messaging from a mobile device, the keyboard
is critical; otherwise, it's difficult to type and send much of a message.
And with our thumbs doing the typing, we risk ergonomic injuries
from overusing that appendage. That's why a portable, foldup external keyboard may be the best solution if you don't have access to the
next big mobile application—voice-text messaging.

Product Tip: Foldup External Keyboard

Stowaway Keyboards are wireless, small foldup keyboards. There are different keyboards designed for the major mobile operating systems. Think Outside Corp., www.thinkoutside.com

Tip: Save Keystrokes

Use Net lingo to save keystrokes and your thumbs. Net lingo uses abbreviations and acronyms to speed up communication. (For more information, see Chapter 5.)

Tip: Phone Calls and Text Messages During a Disaster

There's one other facet of text messaging that's very important. In the event of a disaster, a text message may have a better chance of getting through than a cell call because text messages travel on the portion of a cellphone network that is reserved for data. If a cellular network is overloaded, a cell call can just be dropped; however, a text message just waits its turn in a queue as do emails.

As for voice-text messaging, nicknamed *bubble talk* by its creators, you don't phone someone. Instead, you send a voice message via SMS text messaging that the recipient can hear. That saves your thumbs from doing the talking because your voice mail message is wrapped inside the text message format.

MMS (*Multimedia Messaging Service*) lets you exchange multimedia messages (audio, pictures and video) over wireless networks.

"Browsing" Without an Internet Browser Using Text Messaging

If your cellphone or other mobile device can do text messaging, you have a wealth of information at your fingertips *even if your device does not have an Internet browser.*

If you text the word *help* or the word *tips* and send it to 46645 (which is the first five letters of "Google" on your mobile device dial pad/keyboard), Google will respond with a number of information options such as *directions, movie name, weather, stock ticker, Q&A, Froogle, Google* and *Calculator.*

If you text a sports message (such as the name of your favorite team) to 44636 (which is "4info"), you can get sports scores from www.4info.net.

And if you want to ask *almost anything*, try out AskMeNow's *AskAnything* service. It can answer almost any question where the answer can be found on the Internet. You must sign up at the website before asking questions. Ask a question by calling 888/EZ-ASK ME (which is 888/392-7563) or if you have a BlackBerry, email from your mobile device using the downloadable AskMeNow application. You'll get the answer via a text message or if you have a BlackBerry, via email. Ocean West Holding Corp., www.askmenow.com

Tip: Browse the Web Even With a Dumb Phone

You may be able to do more than text messaging with your phone. It used to be that only smartphones could browse the Web. Now there's *Opera Mini*, a fast and easy program for mobile phones that allows users to access the Web on mobile phones that would normally be incapable of running a Web browser. This includes the vast majority of today's WAP-enabled phones. Instead of requiring the phone to process Web pages, it uses a remote server to pre-process the page before sending it to the phone. This makes Opera Mini perfect for phones with very low resources or low bandwidth connections. Opera Software, ASA
www.opera.com/products/mobile/operamini

Since phone calls may still be a big part of your day, check out Chapter 8 to see how this old-fashioned method of communication is undergoing a revolution.

8

VoIP, Phone Calls and Voice Mail

Now when you dance with someone and then ask for a telephone number, you can't tell what city or state they live in if they have an Internet phone number. That's just one way computers are changing everyday life including how we make and receive phone calls.

Expanding Mobile Content

The content for cellphones and other mobile devices keeps expanding. Besides phone calls, IM and text messaging, many devices let you:

- Get podcasts (through your mobile phone carrier or from software by Pod2mob, www.pod2mob.com/mobile)

- Watch TV (MobiTV, www.mobitv.com) or download to your video iPod or other video player

- Listen to music (Apple, Inc., www.apple.com/itunes)

- Have songs identified (call 866/411-SONG, hold up your handset near the music for 15 seconds and www.zingy.com will text you a message with the artist's name and the song title)

- Get driving directions (Vindigo, Inc., www.vindigo.com)

- Receive restaurant recommendations and more (text Google at 46645; see Chapter 7 for more Google text messaging tips)

VoIP

VoIP (Voice over Internet Protocol) lets you route telephone calls through your broadband (e.g., DSL or cable modem) Internet connection or the connection at many Wi-Fi hot spots. *Video calling* using VoIP is becoming more common as is *audioconferencing* (conference calls). So is *spit* (*sp*am over *I*nternet *T*elephony).

Mobile VoIP phones that combine Wi-Fi and VoIP capabilities can let you make calls without a computer through a wireless Internet access point. Whichever VoIP service you get, make sure it offers strong authentication (passwords or PINs) and encryption security.

Product Tips: VoIP Services
Skype, Skype Limited (a subsidiary of eBay, Inc.), www.skype.com

Vonage, Vonage The Broadband Phone Company, www.vonage.com

Six Reasons for VoIP's Popularity

1. VoIP has features not available on conventional phone service.

With VoIP, you can choose an area code; you're not restricted to just your local area code. You can also take your phone number and access it while on vacation or during a temporary or permanent move to anywhere in the world where there's a broadband Internet connection.

Tip: Virtual Phone Numbers

With VoIP you can have virtual phone numbers. If your company has a large number of clients or customers say in Boston and Seattle, you could have a virtual phone number for each area code. That way calls *to* your company and *from* you would be local calls, not long-distance calls.

2. **VoIP can save you money.**
   There are low-cost or no-cost long-distance and international calling plans.

3. **Voice mail retrieval is flexible.**
   With VoIP, you can check your voice mail by phone, by receiving an email with a message as a sound file or by logging onto the virtual phone company's website and listening to your messages over your computer.

4. **VoIP may be your lifeline during an emergency.**
   When cellular service isn't working, you may still be able to make calls through an Internet-connected computer.

5. **You can multitask.**
   You can still use your computer for other tasks while you're on a VoIP call.

6. **More hot spots are offering VoIP access.**

Warning: The Potential Downsides of VoIP

The potential negatives of VoIP are:

- Problems with your broadband service mean problems with your phone calls.

- Enhanced 911 *may* not be available to help locate a phone's location in case of an emergency.

- Your home alarm security system may need to connect to a traditional phone service.

- A slower or shared Internet connection can affect the audio and video quality.

- Faxing with VoIP is not always as reliable as using a landline.

- A loss of power generally means no phone service unlike traditional landline phones (using the older copper wires), cellphones or satellite phones which can work even if the power is off.

- Some telephone and cable companies are restricting VoIP phone calls, not allowing them or reserving the right to prohibit them in the future.

- If you want your existing phone number to become your VoIP phone number, you could run into difficulties if there isn't an *interconnection agreement* in place between your VoIP provider and the traditional carrier. Ask before you sign up for VoIP service. Also find out how long it will take for the transfer to be completed.

- If your telephone headset is based on Hi-Fi standards and not on telecommunications standards, you could suffer temporary or permanent hearing damage.

- Most importantly, you could have security and privacy issues using the Internet as the mode of transmission. Think of VoIP as spoken email, not necessarily as a secure landline call. More secure systems separate voice and data traffic. Specific virus, spyware and hacker protections may be needed to protect VoIP applications and data firewalls may not be set up to protect voice applications. On the other hand, some VoIP services provide encryption for voice calls and IM between VoIP users. Think about your phone, too. Not all phone instruments offer strong authentication and encryption security.

Seven Ways to Save Time on Phone Calls

Whether you make or receive phone calls with traditional phone service or VoIP, phone calls can still be a big drain on your time and a big source of disrupting interruptions. Walkie-talkie phones with *push-to-talk* technology can make you too available, just like with instant messaging. As with IM, you can better maintain control with a *buddy list* and by using icons to indicate your unavailability (a red "X" for do not disturb). Here's how to make your telephone time work best for you, no matter what kind of phone service you're using:

1. **Determine if phoning is the best way to communicate.**
   If it's more one-way communication from you rather than a dialogue you want to have, see whether email, text messaging or a fax would better meet your needs and save time. Or try calling a person's landline at nonpeak times to leave a voice message.

2. **Plan the timing of your calls and the numbers you call.**
   The busiest time for business calls is usually Monday morning, between 9 and 11 a.m. Sometimes calling before 9 a.m. or after 5 p.m. on weekdays is a good time to catch those hard-to-reach people.

   These days, with cellphones and endless work hours, you often have a good chance of reaching people if you're calling their cell number.

3. **Control the length and scope of the conversation whether you're making or receiving the call.**
   Whether making or receiving a call, indicate your time limits up front (e.g., "I've got five minutes to talk"). Second, clarify the purpose and topic(s). If you're calling, say, "I'd like to discuss these two questions." If you're on the receiving end, ask for clarification if the topic is unclear or the caller seems to be rambling.

4. **Have more outgoing than incoming calls, if possible.**
   If you make more outgoing calls, you can save time because you can better control the timing and agenda of calls. Set up telephone appointments for important calls to cut down on telephone tag time. Since switching activities can slow us down, prioritize and consolidate all callbacks.

5. **Plan the content of your most important calls.**
   If your calls are focused and cover all the essentials, you'll reduce time on the phone as well as the need for callbacks. Prepare for important calls by *writing down* in advance the key questions or areas to cover.

6. **Do something worthwhile when left on hold too long.**
   Turn downtime into productive time. While you're on hold can be a great time to organize your emails by deleting unnecessary ones and filing more important ones.

7. **Take the next step.**
   A big time waster is not remembering information and spending time to retrace steps to trigger a memory. Right after a phone call, write down or type in key points and take any necessary follow-up steps such as transferring information to your calendar or listing the next action step in your PIM or mobile device.

Saving Time on Voice Mail

You can save time handling your voice mail, too, with these tips.

Incoming Calls to Your Voice Mail

1. **Have the right outgoing message.**
   There are four essential elements to a successful outgoing message: (1) give your callers a short time limit (e.g., 60 seconds) on messages they leave and tell them how long they have to leave a message; (2) ask callers to indicate the level of urgency as to when they need to hear back from you; (3) ask callers to leave their phone number two times; and (4) have callers give you the best time to call them back (and if necessary, indicate their time zone or location) to prevent telephone tag.

2. **Let them know how often and when you respond to messages.**
   Let callers know if you are going to have a policy of checking voice mail at set times so you can take control of your time,

energy and schedule and reduce frustration for callers.

Outgoing Calls to Someone Else's Voice Mail

1. Make them *want* to return your call.

Only one in four calls is returned. When making a call to someone else's voice mail, convey what's in it for the person to return your call.

2. Leave the right message.

Indicate *how* and *when* (or even if) you'd like the person to communicate back with you. If you prefer email, let them know that and also leave your email address.

Be sure to leave your name and number (at the beginning and end of your call), a brief message that indicates the purpose of your call and any urgency in returning your call or taking a certain action. Let them know the best times to reach you.

Bypassing Automated Phone Systems to 'Get a Human' at Large Companies

If you want to speak with a human being at some of the largest companies and not to a computer voice-recognition or other automated system designed to push your buttons, see whether Paul English's IVR (interactive voice response) cheat sheet ("The gethuman.com index to customer service quality") at http://gethuman.com has the right buttons for you to push so you can speak to a person. Paul English is the CTO of Kayak.com, the travel search engine.

Phones aren't the only electronic devices we're using to reach out into the world. The next two chapters talk about better ways to use the Internet and the World Wide Web.

Part 3

Mix and Mingle

Searching the World Wide Web

9

Searching the Web: Search Tools and Safety

Imagine you're at a dance and there are billions of potential dance partners there. How can you find the right partner before the dance ends or before you're too old to dance? That's what the World Wide Web (the Web) is like. You don't care that there are billions and billions of pages of information out there—you just want to find the right one for you.

The Difference Between the Internet and the World Wide Web

The Internet (the Net) is a federation of more than a billion computers in a network of networks around the world. Once your computer is connected to the Internet, it can communicate with other computers on the Net through email or instant messaging.

The Web is part of the Internet. It is a way of sharing and accessing information over the Internet. Your browser (such as Internet Explorer) accesses linked Web documents (known as Web pages) including text, images, sound and video.

In the last 10 years, the amount of information traveling over the Internet has grown three thousand percent. There are tens of billions of pages on the Web and it just keeps growing. At best, most search tools are aware of only a percentage of those pages. Even if you combine all the search tools that exist, together they probably cover less than 50 percent of the Web.

Finding and making use of pertinent information can become a job in itself and can create information overload. Searching the Web can also really gobble up your time.

Because the scope of the Web is so vast and time is so short, you need better, faster, safer and more organized ways to find, capture and tap the wealth of information out there.

There are two parts to successfully search the Web. First, as you'll discover in this chapter, is ensuring reliability, Internet privacy and safety and then identifying the best search tools — including essential browser features as well as search engines, toolbars, directories and RSS feeds. Then, in Chapter 10, you'll see specific tips, techniques, software and sites to fine-tune your searches and help you capture, organize, save and retrieve your search results.

Online Warning

Whenever you go online, you can open yourself up to all kinds of problems — such as infecting your computer or network with spyware or a virus that can allow a hacker access to sensitive company or personal information. Although there are virtually no online activities or services that guarantee absolute privacy, Chapters 2 and 3 and this chapter cover essential steps to help protect your computer, mobile devices, information and yourself.

Internet Safety, Privacy and Protection

Every time you go to websites, those sites may be collecting personal or demographic information. A Federal Trade Commission study revealed that 93 percent of online businesses collect personal information and 57 percent gather demographic information from users.

Protect Your Privacy

Besides the security measures discussed in Chapters 2 and 3 including routers, firewalls, antivirus, antispyware and antispam programs, there are four more ways you can protect your privacy:

1. Use one screen name/email address just for browsing.

If your ISP (Internet Service Provider) or email program gives you several screen names or email addresses, use just one for browsing and/or posting to newsgroups so your business or personal in-box won't be flooded with spam or other email that you don't need or want.

2. Read the privacy policies on websites.

Examine privacy policies so you don't inadvertently consent to downloads or the placement of spyware on your computer.

3. Look for website safety certifications.

Two main watchdog groups, BBBOnline (www.bbbonline.com) and TRUSTe (www.truste.org), certify select websites.

4. Search the Web anonymously using stealth software.

Also see hot spots and VPNs in Chapter 2.

Product Tips: Anonymous Internet Surfing Software

Anonymous Surfing helps shield your IP address and protect you from online tracking, pharming attacks and snoops. The always-on 128-bit SSL (Secure Socket Layer) encryption is designed to prevent outside eyes from seeing any data sent to or from your computer. Anonymizer, Inc., 888/270-0141 [CA] or www.anonymizer.com

GhostSurf is a Net surfing tool designed to provide an anonymous, encrypted Internet connection and erase traces of your surfing. Tenebril, Inc., 800/790-9060 [CA] or www.tenebril.com

Cookies

As mentioned in Chapter 2, a *cookie* is a block of text placed in a file on your hard drive by a website when you visit the site. That cookie is then used to identify your computer the next time you access the site and to remember who you and your computer are. Some cookies track your movements on the Internet with or sometimes without your knowledge or permission.

Some cookies are worse than others. A *PIE* (*Persistent Identification Element*) cookie can be tricky to deal with because it makes backups of itself and may come back even after it has been deleted.

Don't Accept All the Cookies You See

Don't let your computer automatically accept cookies. Set your Internet browser to block or at least warn you before letting your computer automatically accept *third party cookies* (cookies not from the site itself).

For the cookies you've accepted, delete those cookies on your computer ideally at least once a day. While you're at it, clean out not just the cookies from your browsing but also your Internet *history* folder (which shows all the sites you've visited) and your *cache* folder, a temporary storage area for pages and images you've visited. These items are stored in different locations, depending on which Internet browser you use. With Internet Explorer 6, go to *Tools* and then

Internet Options to delete *Cookies, Files* and your *History*. Antispyware programs (discussed in Chapter 3) as well as cookie manager programs can often help you do all of these steps automatically. Internet Explorer 7 (which is in beta testing at the time this book is being written) will include a one-step procedure to clear out this information.

Product Tip: Cookie Manager Program
Cookie Pal is a cookie manager to consider for your Web searches. Kookaburra Software, www.kburra.com

Browser Safety Rankings
A browser feature that will become more common in time is a browser's ranking of each website's safety. We'd take those rankings as a starting point for sites to avoid. But someone else's ranking of safety is no substitute for common sense on your part and a bit of healthy caution even on the sites that aren't ranked as dangerous.

Product Tips: Antiphishing Software
Cloudmark Anti-Fraud Toolbar is designed to handle many tasks: display a safety rating for websites; alert you before entering a dangerous site; provide real-time protection against online fraud and identity theft; block spam; and help provide phishing protection as you search the Web or check your Web-based email. Cloudmark, Inc., 415/543-1220 [CA] or www.cloudmark.com

Netcraft Toolbar helps protect you against phishing attacks. The toolbar blocks you from entering a site if the site is a known phishing site looking to harvest your information and maybe your identity. It also lets you know how long the site has been monitored and the country where the site is running. It's available for Internet Explorer and Firefox browsers. Netcraft, Ltd., http://toolbar.netcraft.com

Some browsers already have phishing protection. There will be a phishing protection feature in Internet Explorer 7.

Choosing the Right Internet Connection and Service

Depending on your budget, your needs and the type of service available in your area, you'll either have a dial-up or a high-speed Internet connection (such as DSL, a cable modem or an EV-DO, EDGE or HSDPA wireless broadband access card). Once you've experienced a high-speed connection, you'll never want to go back to dial-up.

Tip: Benefits from a Fast Net Connection

A faster connection can not only make you more productive in finding information, it can also speed up the downloading of files and essential protective updates for your operating system and your antivirus, antispyware and other software programs. The easier and quicker it is for you to handle these housekeeping tasks, the more likely and more often you'll do them.

16 Questions to Ask Before You Sign Up for Internet Service

Ask your ISP (Internet Service Provider):

1. What is the average speed of other users in the same area (building or neighborhood) at different times of the day and night (especially those times when you'll be using the service the most)?

2. What is the guaranteed minimum speed for *uploading* (sending) and *downloading* (receiving) files (a) at your home or business and (b) if nationwide wireless broadband access is offered, anywhere in the country?

3. Is it a shared connection or a dedicated, separate connection?

4. If it's shared, how much can the speed drop due to the number of other customers online at the same time and/or the amount of their usage?

5. Is connecting up to the ISP a local, long distance or toll-free call or no extra cost at all?

6. Are there any limits on how much you can download during any given time period?

7. How much online storage is provided for emails? Photos? Files?

8. Are virus protection and spam blocking built into the ISP software?

9. What has been the average and also the longest downtime for customers during the past three months, six months and one year when the service was not working?

10. What is the average response time for solving problems?

11. Is 24x7 technical support included?

12. Is a backup dial-up connection included in the cost if the "high-speed" service goes down and becomes a "no-speed" service?

13. Are VoIP phone calls restricted now? Can they be in the future under the agreement?

14. Is there a free trial period of say 30 days where there is no charge for the modem or the installation and cancellation can be for any reason or no reason?

15. Is there a month-to-month agreement or one for a fixed, longer term to use the service?

16. Can the service be cancelled at any time if the service deteriorates to what a *customer* deems to be an unacceptable degree (such as too slow a connection speed or too much downtime)?

And, of course, be sure the Internet Service Provider sends you a confirming email as to these items so you'll have them in writing.

Choosing the Right Web Browser and Features

Even if you think your current *Web browser* (the software application you use to locate and display Web pages) is working just fine for you,

you may want to consider using a different browser, more than one browser or extra browser add-ons. Browsers have different features that may appeal to you or turn you off. For example, Firefox helps you search a Web page on your screen through *word wheeling* where it searches and matches text as you type.

Hacker Attracters

If a browser or operating system is more widely used, it's a more attractive target to hackers. But no browser or operating system is totally immune from attacks. A smaller target can still be a target. As BBC commentator Bill Thompson said, "Security through obscurity is no security at all." And if a less-used browser increases in popularity, then it may become a more attractive target over time.

With browser security on everyone's front burner, it's also important to consider not only the frequency and severity of attacks but also the efforts being made by each browser provider to improve its overall security architecture as well as its speed in issuing patches (fixes) for security problems. Whichever browser you use, it is vital to regularly (and, if possible, automatically) download browser security updates to help prevent security issues.

Tabbed Browsing

Browsers that offer tabbed browsing may make your daily Web experience much more productive.

With *tabbed browsing* all it takes is *one click* to open up (and keep open) all of your favorite websites and/or bookmarks in tabs *on one page* rather than on multiple, separate pages.

How Tabbed Browsing Works

With tabbed browsing, you load up many websites at one time and save them (permanently if you want) as tabs. What's the advantage? Whenever you go on the Web with the browser, the websites are automatically loaded up and appear on your screen as tabs that you can click to instantly retrieve their Web pages. The benefit is that you have all the tabbed sites on call, just a click away, whenever you need them, rather than going out to the websites each time you need them and waiting for the Web pages to load up. You can add (or delete) sites or bookmarks as tabs at any time.

You may still need to use your regular browser on some sites because not all tabbed browsers currently work on every site.

Product Tips: Web Browsers with Tabbed Browsing

Firefox, Mozilla Foundation, www.mozilla.org/products/firefox/

Mozilla, Mozilla Foundation, www.mozilla.org

NetCaptor, Stilesoft Inc., www.netcaptor.com

Opera, Opera Software ASA, www.opera.com

Apple's Safari browser is a tabbed browser. Internet Explorer 7 (in beta testing at the time this book is being written) will be a tabbed browser.

Bookmarking Favorite Web Pages

Bookmarking is an alternative or adjunct to tabbed browsing and it comes with virtually every browser. You simply create a list of your favorite Web pages so you can just click on their names from your *Favorites* list to link to the Web page or website to retrieve it. Here's how you can bookmark (add a site to your list): with your browser on the screen, go to one of your favorite sites, click *Favorite* and then click *Add*. That should do it or some variation of these steps for your browser.

Use Multiple Windows With or Without Tabbed Browsing

Whether or not your browser has tabbed browsing, you can still save some time switching between different sites or links by opening up several windows at a time. Instead of linking to a site by clicking on a link with the left mouse button (which removes the current Web page from the screen), click with the *right* mouse button, which in Internet Explorer 6, for example, brings up the option *Open in New Window*.

In Internet Explorer as you open up each new window with the right mouse button, the previous window is replaced on the screen by the new window. However, the previous window now has a button on the task bar at the bottom of your screen showing the name of the Web page. You can switch between windows by clicking on the buttons.

Another option is to open windows through (a) the *File* menu (and clicking *Open*) or (b) the blank address box at the top. Then simply type in each website or Web page URL and tap the *Return* key. Before you open a new Web page in a new window, *minimize* the current window (by clicking on the minus in the upper right of the window) and the window will disappear from the screen but leave a button on the task bar. Once again, you can use the task bar to click on the buttons to switch between multiple windows because each window is represented by a button on the task bar. You could also hold down *Alt* and then tap *Tab* to rotate through the open windows.

(See also information on multiple windows in Chapter 10.)

RSS Feeds and More

RSS stands for *Really Simple Syndication* and it turns your computer into a type of ticker-tape machine that automatically receives news feeds or other content in your areas of interest from websites. This can save you time because the news and information are *pushed* (automatically sent) to your computer's screen rather than making you spend time going out on the Web to find it.

If you want to keep track of a large number of news-related or other content websites, you may want to get a browser with a built-in RSS system (such as the tabbed browser Firefox) or have a browser add-on with an RSS system that works with your browser. Internet Explorer 7 will include integrated RSS along with tabbed browsing and the next version of Outlook will integrate RSS feeds with emails.

We expect the uses for RSS feeds will continue to expand to include sending emails, private workgroup collaboration, calendar items and reminders, shopping deals and whatever other non-news content you want flowed automatically to your screen or desktop. By the way, the RSS term is sometimes also referred to as *Web feeds*.

Product Tips: RSS Systems

Bloglines is a free online service that helps you subscribe to and manage Web information such as news feeds, weblogs (blogs) and audio. This Web-based service can be used from any computer or mobile device with a Web browser. Bloglines is a *news aggregator*—it tracks the information you're interested in from many online information sources including websites, blogs and news services; retrieves new information as it happens; and organizes everything for you on your own personal Web news page. IAC Search & Media, www.bloglines.com

FeedDemon is a standalone RSS reader with a built-in tabbed browser. It is preconfigured with dozens of popular feeds and lets you create "watches" where stories with your keywords in the news are automatically sent to you. This RSS reader allows you to organize information in different ways and it has a built-in podcast receiver and many more features. NewsGator Technologies, Inc., www.newsgator.com

FeedForAll allows you to easily create, edit and publish RSS feeds. NotePage, Inc., www.feedforall.com

Feed Scout offers more than 100 predefined news feeds in 10 predefined categories. It appears as a toolbar in Internet Explorer and new RSS feeds can be discovered and added. ByteScout Software Development, www.bytescout.com

Product Tip: Create Your Own Online Newspaper

TotalNews lets you assemble a personalized online newspaper by pulling stories and news from newspapers and

TV news sites you designate and putting the information on a personalized online news page. TotalNews, www.totalnews.com

RSS and Podcast Security Warning
As RSS has become more popular, hackers are now producing RSS spam and potentially more dangerous RSS malware. The more security-conscious RSS news aggregators, readers and podcatchers help control malware by filtering, screening and authenticating files, including warnings on certain file types and/or requiring end user intervention for each download. (For more on podcasts, see Chapter 10.)

Customizing Your Browser
There are many ways you can customize the appearance of your browser from changing the text size and the font type to making Web pages easier to read. (One no-cost font-enlarging solution that works with some websites as well as the listing of search engine results, is holding down the Ctrl [Control] key and rolling the scrolling wheel on your mouse to adjust the font size.) Some browsers, such as Opera, have a zoom feature. (Internet Explorer 7 will have a zoom feature.)

Product Tips: Font Enlarging Software
Liquid Surf customizes the appearance of Web content by allowing you to increase or decrease the size of text and graphics within Internet Explorer. Portrait Displays, Inc., 925/227-2700 [CA] or www.portrait.com

Web Eyes is an Internet Explorer plug-in that allows you to instantly change the text size and font of any website you visit. With one click of the "Read Like a Book" icon, your scrolling document converts to a book format. You simply turn the page instead of scrolling to have a more natural reading experience and increase your reading efficiency. ION Systems, Inc., www.webeyes.us

Choosing the Right Home Page

When you click on your browser to start it and connect to the Internet, your browser goes to a home page. This is your starting point each day when you start (or restart) your browser or exit a particular Web page and just want to return *home* within your browser.

Start the day out right and quickly by picking a home page that loads quickly (i.e., has a lot of bandwidth and not too many graphics). A search engine page such as Google (www.google.com) fits both of these categories and also lets you have a Web search tool right on the screen.

The steps to change your home page depend on which browser you are using. In Internet Explorer 6, you select your home page by opening up the browser; going to *Tools* and then *Internet Options*; typing in the *new home page URL* (e.g., www.google.com) in the box to the right of Address; and clicking *Enter*.

The Evolution of Web Search Tools

Just as the features and names of mobile devices are morphing, converging and expanding in scope, so are the Web search tools.

There used to be very distinct categories such as directories, search engines and Web databases. Now the distinctions are blurring as search sites keep up with their competition.

Alchemy and the Ultimate Search Tool

Currently, search tools are excellent at finding specific facts (e.g., the population of the United States) or pointing you in the right direction for broader questions or topics by giving you a list of sites (in one continuous list, in organized folders or with visual maps) that should contain what you're trying to find.

The Holy Grail of future searching tools will be one that provides a one sentence or paragraph narrative answer to a detailed question rather than producing a list of thousands of Web pages that you have to sift through to find the answer. This will be the alchemy of the Digital Information Age—turning information into gold. The good news is that a lot of this technology is available now.

The trend is for search tools to:

1. Remember what you like to search for to have faster repeated searches over time

2. Automatically update those searches on preset intervals (e.g., hourly, daily or weekly)

3. Push information in your areas of interest automatically to your mobile device or computer screen

4. Create both summarized and detailed, annotated search results that you can easily import into an email, an instant message, a text message, a word processing or spreadsheet document or an online presentation or document

5. Suggest new areas of inquiry as artificial intelligence allows your *bot* (robot) search tool to "think"

The Top Search Tools

In addition to automatic updating Web page software covered in Chapter 10 and RSS feeds discussed earlier in this chapter, these are six other top search tools:

1. Search engines

2. Metasearch engines

3. Specialized search engines

4. Search toolbars

5. Metasearch toolbars

6. Directories

The best search tool depends on what you're searching for and how much specific information you already have to speed up your search.

Traditional Search Engines for More Specific Searches

When you think of a tool to search the Web, what generally comes to mind is a traditional *search engine* such as Google (www.google.com).

A search engine is useful for finding an answer based on particular words, bits of information or even specific questions, unlike a *directory* (see below) which is generally better suited for subjects that can be put into broader categories. Generally, a search engine gives you a list of links (website addresses) where the information you want should be found.

The key to using a traditional search engine isn't coming up with websites to look at; it's determining which sites are worth your time to investigate. Often, you'll get way too many results when you search. That's why using more specific search words and advanced search commands will speed up and narrow your quest. (See Chapter 10 for tips on how to improve such searches on the Web.)

Product Tip: Create Your Own Search Engine
Rollyo lets you create a custom search engine that can search (1) only sites you specify, (2) "searchrolls" shared by others or (3) the entire Web. (The site is in beta testing at the time this book is being written.) Rollyo, www.rollyo.com

Product Tip: Search with a "Matching" Engine and a Search Engine
PubSub isn't a search engine—it's a matching engine that's a complement to search engines. Traditional search engines do a search of the past—whatever has already been published on the Web and indexed in the search engine's database. They're like a still photograph that records one moment. PubSub is like a camera that keeps taking snapshots. PubSub does a search of the future, called *prospective search*, as compared to a *retrospective search* which searches the past. The site maintains a list of your search requests and matches them in real time

against new documents as they appear in the future on the Web. It's a cross between an RSS feed and a search engine. You can get search results via Internet (including email), SMS, PDA/mobile devices and IM networks. PubSub currently reads over 20 million weblogs, more than 50,000 Internet newsgroups and all SEC (EDGAR) filings. PubSub will be adding more streams of data over time. PubSub Concepts, Inc., www.pubsub.com

Product Tip: Try a Wiki (Community) Search Engine

Prefound.com is a human-indexed search engine that only searches Web pages that other members of the Web community have saved and tagged (labeled). This "wiki search engine" also lets you share the great links you've found. iLOR, LLC, www.prefound.com

Product Tips: Traditional Search Engines

Although all of these search engines are valuable, they differ in their ranking techniques, search techniques and the number of Web pages included in their indexes. For a more detailed look at the pros and cons of each search engine, go to *www.searchenginewatch.com* and click on the *Search Ratings and Stats* and also the *Search Engines Resources*.

AlltheWeb, www.alltheweb.com

AltaVista, www.altavista.com

Ask.com, www.ask.com

Google, www.google.com

HotBot, www.hotbot.com

Lycos, www.lycos.com

MSN, www.search.msn.com

Yahoo!, www.yahoo.com

Search Site Warning

Some Web search sites let advertisers pay to be included in search results and some don't. Some indicate which results are paid for and some don't.

Privacy Warning

As mentioned in Chapter 2, Internet search engines generally store your search terms and search history forever. As search engine companies expand their product offerings (e.g., free email accounts, online groups and online photo storage), they are also gathering your name, address and other kinds of *personally identifiable information* about you that they could link up with your search history.

All of this collected information could possibly become available not only to hackers if they penetrated search engine security defenses but also to the government and maybe even to litigants in civil cases (such as divorces). You can help protect the privacy of your Internet searches with products such as *Anonymous Surfing* (www.anonymizer.com) if you use all of its encrypting and hiding features.

Widgets and Gadgets

Widgets and *Gadgets* are small programs that run on your desktop independently of a browser. They are used for tasks such as showing the weather or traffic maps or getting RSS feeds. They are becoming essential, handy tools as they expand in the scope of information they provide.

Metasearch Engines for Simultaneous Searches

With a metasearch engine, you can do a simultaneous search of several search engines at the same time. You type in the keyword(s) in the search box and the metasearch engine transmits your search simultaneously to several search engines and their databases of Web pages. The results cover all the search engines queried.

Metasearch engines do not have their own database of Web pages. Instead, they transmit your search terms to the databases maintained by search engine companies. Because metasearch engines search many search engines at once, this gives a broader search but not necessarily a more focused one.

Product Tips: Metasearch Engines

Copernic Agent lets you simultaneously search more than 90 search engines grouped into 10 categories. Copernic Technologies, Inc., www.copernic.com

Dogpile is another popular metasearch engine. InfoSpace, Inc., www.dogpile.com

MrSapo Search World takes a different approach. From one window listing the various search engines, you can see the results of each search engine individually, one at a time. Then just click a button on the next search engine and you can see the results of that search engine. Intelways Network, www.mrsapo.com

Web's Biggest says it searches more domain names than any other search engine. Web's Biggest, LLC, www.websbiggest.com

Specialized Search Engines

Specialized (*vertical*) niche search engines are becoming increasingly important as the number of Web pages keeps multiplying. Many specialized search engines have access to their own Web databases. Since the goal of searching is finding the correct information quickly, these search engines can help you zero in on the needed data or answers.

Product Tips: Specialized Search Engines

Become.com is a shopping search site that also shows product reviews. Become, Inc., www.become.com

CorporateInformation gives you information on private and foreign companies from 58 countries. Wrights Investors' Service, www.corporateinformation.com

Daypop searches 59,000 news sites plus weblogs and RSS feeds. Daypop, www.daypop.com

Hoover's Online has good free and fee info on 14,000 companies. Hoovers, Inc., www.hoovers.com

NewsLibrary searches over 700 U.S. newspapers and other sources and charges per article. News Bank, Inc., www.newslibrary.com

Search Toolbars

Another approach you can use for Web searches is a search toolbar which adds a search box to your browser. This small toolbar can be on your screen all the time, no matter which other program you're using. This can be a real time saver because it lets you do searches without having to switch applications or launch a Web browser. The toolbar usually includes a pop-up blocker, too.

Privacy Warning

There can be a privacy issue with toolbars, though, because they allow search sites to track your online activity. Search sites can do that already but not all of them track and record your searching. You may want to investigate this privacy issue before you sign up for a search toolbar and also see whether the tracking feature can be disabled.

Product Tip: Search Toolbar

Google Toolbar does more than website searches. The Toolbar 4 Beta lets you share Web pages via email, text messaging or blogging; display syndicated feeds; convert U.S. street addresses into links on online maps; access your bookmarks from any computer; create custom search buttons; get suggestions from the Toolbar on search phrases; and more. Google, Inc., www.toolbar.google.com

Metasearch Toolbars

Just as a metasearch engine does a simultaneous search of several search engines, so does a metasearch toolbar.

Product Tips: Metasearch Toolbars

Copernic Meta, Copernic Technologies, Inc., www.copernic.com

Dogpile, InfoSpace, Inc., www.dogpile.com

Directories for Broader, Categorized Searches

A directory is more suited for researching broader topics and more general questions. A directory gives you a hierarchical list of websites in the categories and subcategories you need to explore.

When you use a directory, you don't look for a specific word; you look for a topic or subject. To explore that topic, you *drill down* (click) your way through various categories and narrower subcategories to where you'll find lists of websites on different subjects related to your topic.

Search engines and directories are put together in different ways. A search engine uses computers to put together the sites to search. Directories are compiled and organized by *taxonomists*, people whose job it is to search the Web and create these categories and subcategories of sites.

Product Tips: Directories

Business.gov is a business directory with a wide range of business topics.
U.S. Business Advisor, www.business.gov

Open Directory is the largest, most comprehensive human-edited directory of the Web. It is constructed and maintained by a vast, global community of volunteer editors. www.dmoz.org

Yahoo! is the most well-known directory. Yahoo, Inc., www.yahoo.com

Searching with Mobile Devices

Due to the popularity of personal electronic devices, search services are specially developing tools for mobile devices.

Tip: Mobile Search Services

For example, Google has a Mobile Web search service (*http://mobile.google.com/*) that only links to pages that are formatted to display properly on the small screens of mobile devices with a Web browser. Google has another mobile search service for phones that don't have a Web browser but do have WML (wireless markup language). Google also has a limited search service for phones that do text messaging with SMS through which you send a text question to Google at 46645 (Googl). Unsure if your phone has SMS? Text a message to Google at 46645 and if you get an answer, you've got it! (For more information on texting Google, see Chapter 7.)

It's just a matter of time until virtually any mobile device will have the capability to do full Web browsing and searching using products such as *Opera Mobile* or *Opera Mini* (www.opera.com).

To better use these search tools, read on in Chapter 10—Searching the Web 2.0—for specific search tips as well as products to help you organize, save and retrieve your search results and tap the knowledge of the Web's community.

10

Searching the Web 2.0: Software, Sites and Tips

There's a certain etiquette or protocol on the dance floor and on the Internet, too.

Internet Protocol (IP) is the method for sending information from one computer to another over the Net. Every computer on the Internet has an IP address that uniquely identifies it from all other computers on the Net. When you retrieve data from Web pages, that data is broken up into packets of information that are transmitted through various gateways until they end up on your computer screen with your IP address.

But even though you may not be interested in *how* information reaches your screen, you do want better and faster ways to search, organize, save and retrieve that information. New products and approaches are continually being developed.

In the last chapter, you saw the browsers, search tools and protection to have on hand. In this chapter, you'll see software, websites and search tips and techniques to improve your online searching capabilities so you can make the most of your time as well as the information you find.

Capturing, Organizing and Saving Information Found on the Web

Before doing your next Web search, start using some of the following tips and tools to capture, save and organize the information you find so you can easily retrieve and use it in the future.

Web Information Manager Programs

Web information manager software programs can help you:

1. Capture information from the Web in a variety of different ways — for example, a full page with or without graphics or just highlighted sections

2. Speed up the downloading of files

3. Organize information visually or within folders into meaningful categories

4. Easily retrieve and share data

Some Web info managers can capture streaming video and audio and most integrate with search engines to browse and download files.

Product Tips: Web Information Manager Programs

Blinkx.tv allows you to search the Web for video and audio clips and podcasts not only using standard keyword and Boolean queries but also conceptual searches that retrieve content that is conceptually similar to your search text. *Blinkx.tv* also includes Smart Folders which allow you to view, organize and save video clips, audio clips and websites (or just the links) on your computer's hard disk. You can view the contents of a Smart Folder without being connected to the Internet. You can also get rich media content via RSS feeds using Blinkx's SmartFeed RSS API. Blinkx, www.blinkx.tv

Clusty organizes search results into folders with similar items (clusters) grouped together. A search for *blackberry*, for example, will group results into folders such as BlackBerry (the mobile device) and blackberry (the fruit). Vivisimo, Inc., www.clusty.com

Grokker converts search results from text into topically organized categories and subcategories in a map of floating spheres with zoom-in/zoom-out navigation. Each Web link and document features a summary preview balloon that allows you to quickly assess its relevance. You can create a map on any topic, customize it with your own categories and labels, add links, rearrange results and then save it and email it using any email application. Groxis, Inc., 866/968-4765 [CA] or www.groxis.com

Internet Research Scout helps your online research by providing an easy way to search, save and organize information from the Internet. It can be used directly from many leading browsers. You can capture entire HTML pages including images, flash and text and automatically save them to a hard drive with one click; edit and review captured HTML snippets and pages; and export to HTML, MHT or searchable PDF. Bytescout Software Development, www.bytescout.com

Mass Downloader can download individual files (or lists of files) from Web, FTP and HTTPS sites at the maximum available speed. It can also record streaming media (PNM, RTSP and MMS) to your disk. MetaProducts, Corp., www.metaproducts.com

MetaProducts Inquiry allows you to collect, organize, view and save entire Web pages, selected text and images and Shockwave Flash clips. MetaProducts, Corp., www.metaproducts.com/MP/ Inquiry_Standard_Edition.htm

Offline Explorer lets you browse offline by downloading an unlimited number of your favorite Web, FTP and HTTPS sites for later offline viewing, editing or browsing. It can also record streaming media (PNM, RTSP and MMS) to your disk. MetaProducts, Corp., www.metaproducts.com

Onfolio is a PC application that works within Internet Explorer and Firefox to let you (a) collect, organize, search and export online content—including RSS feeds—to email, blogs and websites and (b) review offline entire Web pages, portions of text and pictures. Onfolio, Inc., 888/663-6546 [MA] or www.onfolio.com

SurfSaver lets you save, organize, and search the information you gather on the Internet. askSam Systems, 800/800-1997 [FL] or www.surfsaver.com

Watson 2.0 is a desktop tool that automatically and continuously monitors what you are looking at on the Web or working on in Microsoft Word, PowerPoint, Explorer or Outlook and then returns search results relevant to the context of the Web page or document. The search results come from a combination of search engine results and the files on your computer and/or on a corporate server. As you move through a document or Web page and the context changes, so do the search results. Intellext, Inc., www.intellext.com

Also see Chapter 11 for desktop search programs that can help you quickly find information on one computer or multiple computers.

Summarizing Software

The process of collecting and organizing information can be speeded up by using software to automate the creation of concise summaries of any document or Web page.

Product Tip: Summarizing Software

Copernic Summarizer can analyze text of any length on any subject in any one of four languages and create a summary as short or as long as you want it to be. It can summarize Word documents, Web pages, PDF files and email messages. The *Copernic LiveSummarizer* bundled feature appears as a pane at the bottom of the Internet Explorer window. As you browse the Web, it displays in real time a concise summary of the Web page that is currently open. That way, you may not need to read the entire page to find out if it is useful. Copernic Technologies, Inc., www.copernic.com

Web Page Updating Software

Once you've found a valuable Web page or website, you probably don't have the time to keep going back to see whether any new or updated information has been added. Fortunately, there is software that automatically revisits Web pages and websites you designate and alerts you if there's new information.

Product Tip: Web Page Updating Software

Copernic Tracker monitors Web pages and notifies you when they change. It automatically looks for new content on Web pages you're interested in, as often as you like, and keeps you up to date with what's new on those sites. When a change is detected, it can display a desktop alert or send you an email (and even include a copy of the Web page with the changes highlighted). Copernic Technologies, Inc., www.copernic.com

Search Engine Tips and Techniques

When you search the Web, you're looking for quality, not quantity. The more precise your search words and the more advanced your search techniques, the more time you can save searching.

For any search engine you regularly use, take a look at the *FAQs* (frequently asked questions) or Help option to see special searching tips for that particular engine.

We'll illustrate searching tips and techniques using Google (www.google.com) for the balance of this chapter.

By the way, if you want to access your entire search history with Google to repeat previous searches, add bookmarks to your favorite websites or add labels and notes to them, go to *www.google.com/ searchhistory*. This Personalized Search feature also orders your search results based on what you've searched for in the past.

Top Search Tips

If you just saw a friend using a cool BlackBerry to pick up his email and wanted some info on the device, here are some ways you could search for more information.

Type Search Requests in Lower Case Letters

If you went to www.google.com, typed in *BLACKBERRY* in all upper case letters and clicked *Google Search*, you'd get more than 25 million results. If you did a new search with *blackberry* in all lower case letters, the total number of results would be the same. That's because Google automatically converts search requests to lower case letters to include more possibilities. With search engines in general, type in a search request in all lower case letters to have a broader search because some search engines do not automatically convert to lower case letters. (Although you want fewer possibilities to sort through, you don't want to inadvertently miss any vital ones with an all caps search.)

Keep Your Search Page and Search Results Page(s) in Separate Windows

Ordinarily, when you search with Google, your *search page* is replaced by a *search results page*. If you'd prefer to also keep your main search page open, you can set this preference option to open your search results in a new browser window. For more information, see *http://www.google.com/preferences*

Read a Site's Description Before Clicking to Open It

Clicking on Google's *I'm Feeling Lucky* option takes you directly to the site that Google determines is likely to be the most relevant and correct for your precise search. For safety reasons, we personally prefer to click *Google Search* instead and review the description of the first site on the search results page before we click and take our computers to that website.

> ### Tip: HTML Files
> When you search the Web, be aware that different types of files have different risks. Files in the *HTML* format are less likely to contain a virus. For that reason, results from a Google search will sometimes list a result followed by *View as HTML*. This alternative HTML format is safer for you to select and probably also faster to load.

There's More on the Search Results Page Than Just a List of Web Pages

There's some great information on the results page besides the total number of results and the listing of websites with information. It may be more fruitful to track down your BlackBerry info using this other information rather than clicking on links to websites.

For example, on your BlackBerry search, next to the total number of search results and the word *blackberry* at the top of the page, click on the *definition* link that's underlined. If you scroll down the definition page, you'll not only see definitions for the blackberry fruit, translations of the word blackberry into other languages but also images of the fruit. That's all very interesting but you were on a quest for a mobile device.

Now go back up towards the top of the page and you'll see right below blackberry (plant), "Or did you mean: *BlackBerry (technology)*?"

Click on the *BlackBerry (technology)* link and you'll see quite an extensive description of the BlackBerry devices and features, photos of various models and links to various websites, including the website of the manufacturer of BlackBerry: www.blackberry.com.

Chances are you can find out what you need at www.blackberry.com. But if not, tap the Backspace key on your keyboard or mouseclick the back arrow on the top of the screen to get back to the results page. Take a look at the additional info at the top of the results page.

At the top, above the word in the search box, is an underlined *Images* link. Click on the link and you'll see a large number of photos of BlackBerry devices. Similarly, you can click on other categories such as *Groups*, *News* or *Froogle* (to buy a BlackBerry) and *more*. (As this book is being written, Google is testing a new interface for the results page with the links to Images, Groups, News, Froogle and local search pages appearing on the left instead of on top.)

The *more* link takes you to the Google Services page where, among the list of services you can choose to get, is Google email *Alerts* for news on a topic of interest, such as a BlackBerry mobile device.

If you go back to the search results page, notice that the top right side of the page has entries under the heading of *Sponsored Links*. Companies have paid to be listed on search results pages when someone types in *blackberry*. The good news is that Google clearly separates and indicates which links are sponsored (paid) links. Some search engines mix in paid links with nonpaid links.

Now that you're thinking of getting that BlackBerry for yourself, you better think of getting something your significant other would like, too. How about a vacation in Hawaii?

Type in *Hawaii* and you'll get over 200 million links to look at. You have to be more specific here.

Get Subtraction from Addition

If you make your search request more specific (i.e., search for *Hawaii* and *vacation*), over 90 percent of the Hawaii results are eliminated. Now there are *only* 14 million links but the first half dozen links may contain exactly what you need.

The syntax for adding a search item in Google is either of the following:

Hawaii +vacation

or

Hawaii vacation

Note: With Google, you don't need to type the "and." You may need to do this on other search engines.

Get Subtraction from Subtraction

If you excluded the island Maui from the search quest, more results are eliminated.

You should get this subtraction by typing:

Hawaii +vacation –Maui

Going back to your BlackBerry search, you could have eliminated sites by typing *blackberry –jelly* so you wouldn't see sites talking about blackberry jelly. That would have gotten rid of the jelly sites but not everything related to the blackberry fruit—you still would have seen websites dealing with blackberry cobblers, for example. So, although the minus sign can help pare down the search list, it's often not as useful as adding terms to search for to make the search result more precise.

Avoid Math with the Advanced Search Page

If you hated math classes and don't want to be reminded of it with plusses and minuses, you have a plain English alternative for avoiding the math symbols.

For example, on the main Google search page, to the right of the search request box, there is a link to *Advanced Search*. If you click on that link, you can find search results

- With all of the specified words
- With just an exact phrase and the words exactly in that order
- With at least one of the words
- Without certain words
- With 10, 20, 30, 50 or 100 results per page

- In any language or just a certain language

- In any file format or just a certain format (e.g., Word, HTML, PDF)

- In only certain domains (e.g., just "gov")

- With Web pages that have been updated just within the last three months, six months, year or anytime

- With the search-for words anywhere on the page or just in the title of the page, the text of the page, the URL of the page or links to the page

- With results only from a certain domain (for example, if you were searching for a BlackBerry, you might only want to see results from www.blackberry.com)

- With SafeSearch filtering to eliminate adult explicit sites

- With page-specific searches for Web pages similar to a particular Web page or linked to a specific Web page

- With topic-specific searches such as searching scholarly papers by clicking the link to Google Scholar

Not that we want to encourage cheating, but you can find a Google search cheat sheet and the Google help page respectively at:
www.google.com/help/cheatsheet.html
www.google.com/help/

You can take searching a step further by using Google advanced operators which are query words that have special meaning to Google. These operators generally modify a search in some way or tell Google to do a totally different type of search. The URL for the Google advanced operators page is *www.google.com/help/operators.html*

Learn the ABCs to Refine Your Searches

Many search engines can do some or all of the following:

1. **Translation** of Web pages into another language

2. **Stemming**—this is where a search engine automatically includes

words that (a) share a *stem* (the main part of a word such as *cell* in cellular and cellphone) or (b) are similar to some or all of the search terms

3. **Wildcard searches** where you use *?* for one missing character and *** to show characters or words following the typed-in portion of a word. For example, *math** would also show *mathematics*. An asterisk wildcard in a Google search can also match one or more entire words of text so that the query matches a contiguous sequence of words. For example, a search for *cooking * classes* will match the phrases *cooking school classes* and *cooking and wine tasting classes*. One common use of the asterisk is to fill in the blanks for a query — e.g., *the parachute was invented by **

4. **Showing older, replaced Web pages** — some search engines will show you what a Web page looked like at the time it was originally added to the database. This can give you a snapshot back in time if the page has changed since then.

Choose How to Read the Search Results

Some search engines only display links to one or two pages from each website to let you also quickly see other sites that may be helpful. Sometimes the second page is indented so you can quickly determine that it's from the same site as the one above.

You can click on *More from this site* or *More hits from* or similar terminology to see additional pages. *More from this site* is not the same as *More like this* which may appear in search results. *More like this* will call up other similar pages from various sites.

Search within results or *Search within your results* lets you do a search within a search to focus in on the desired information. The second search is only done within the results of the first search.

Search Tips to Use on a Site

Sometimes you know you're on the right website but you're having difficulty finding the needed information. Here are two good tools to use:

Search with the Find Feature

To find a word or phrase just on the Web page shown on the screen:

1. Hold the *Control key (Ctrl)* and tap the *F key* or click *Find* in the *Edit* menu.

2. Type in the *word or phrase*.

3. Click *Find Next*.

Search with a Toolbar

If the word or phrase you need to find isn't on the Web page on your screen but you think it's somewhere on the website, see if a browser search box toolbar (e.g., Google toolbar at www.toolbar.google.com) has a *Search the site* option. This allows you to find the search item anywhere on a website. This can be very useful when you know you're on the correct website and the needed information is there somewhere. (Some browsers, such as Firefox, have *incremental search* and *smart keywords* that allow you to search within Web pages and websites.)

Selected Content-Specific Sites

Finding Specific Answers

If you're looking for specific answers rather than a listing of sites or links, see whether these websites will give you a quicker answer than a search engine or other search tool described in Chapter 9.

Product Tips: Answers, Not Links

About.com offers practical advice and solutions for everyday life including home repairs, recipes, car buying tips and much more. About.com, www.about.com

AllExperts.com is the oldest and largest free Q&A service on the Internet. AllExperts.com, www.allexperts.com

Answers.com is a reference search service created to provide you with instant answers on over a million topics.

Rather than a standard search engine's approach of giving you a list of links to follow, Answers.com displays quick, snapshot answers from what is described as concise, reliable information taken from over 100 authoritative encyclopedias, dictionaries, glossaries and atlases. Answers Corporation, www.answers.com

Ask.com offers many ways to get answers to your questions. IAC Search & Media, www.ask.com

Babylon.com offers instant translations and definitions of terms and expressions from 25 brand dictionaries in 13 languages and over 40 premium content titles. Babylon.com, Ltd., www.babylon.com

Encyclopedia Brittanica has a wealth of information. www.britannica.com

Infoplease.com has been on the Internet since 1998 as the source of factual answers. Its roots go back to its origination as a radio show in 1938. Pearson Education, www.infoplease.com

Webopedia is an online dictionary and search engine for computer and Internet technology definitions. Jupitermedia Corp., www.webopedia.com

Whonu.com is an interesting online search, research, discovery and idea-generating tool that lets you find information in many different ways—through discovery searches to find facts, tips and how to's; Web searches using the major search engines, directories, groups and forums; articles, images, country and language-specific searches and more. The site is in beta testing at the time this book is being written. Simply Brilliant, Inc., www.whonu.com

Blogs and Vlogs

There are many sites to help you find blogs (weblogs). Search engine solutions to find vlogs (video blogs) keep evolving.

Product Tips: Blog Search Sites

Bloglines is a free online service that helps you subscribe to and manage Web information such as news feeds, blogs and audio. IAC Search & Media, www.bloglines.com

Google Blog Search is a search tool devoted to blogs. Google, Inc., http://blogsearch.google.com

PubSub currently reads over 20 million weblogs, more than 50,000 Internet newsgroups and all SEC (EDGAR) filings. PubSub will be adding more streams of data over time. It's a cross between an RSS feed and a search engine. PubSub Concepts, Inc., www.pubsub.com

Technorati is a real-time search engine that keeps track of what's going on in the blogosphere — the world of weblogs. Technorati, www.technorati.com

And keep a watchful eye for *splogs*—spam blogs.

Web 2.0 Community Searches and Sharing

Web 2.0 is not only part of this chapter's title, it's also a term that refers to the communal, connective aspect of Web searching and sharing. Web 2.0 emphasizes the interconnectedness of the online community—a community that is becoming increasingly personalized and useful as Web users share content, bookmarks and comments/descriptors (known as *tags, tagging* or *folksonomies*). Blogs, wikis and even RSS feeds are or can be forms of this online sharing.

Tags help identify, organize and label content for yourself and/or others by allowing searches for Web pages using the keyword tags. Specialized tag searching engines will become more popular. The tagged pages are stored on the Internet and not on your computer so you can access them from any computer. You can specify tags that can be used just by you, also by other people you designate or by anyone on the Net. (And, once again, spam rears its ugly head with *tag spam*.) A *tag cloud* is a weighted list of tags in a visual format so, for example, the more frequently used tags are in a larger font.

If you want to see sites that other people find useful and maybe want to share your own favorites, take a look at community search and sharing sites.

Product Tips: Community Search and Sharing Sites

Clipmarks lets you highlight, grab (clip), tag, save, organize and share pieces of information from Web pages. Amplify LLC, www.clipmarks.com

del.icio.us is a social bookmarks manager. It allows you to easily add sites you like to your personal collection of links, to categorize those sites with keywords (tags) and to share your collection with others. Yahoo!, Inc., http://del.icio.us

Jeteye lets you share with others a package containing your searches, search results, comments and more. Jeteye Technologies, Inc., www.jeteye.com

Kaboodle is a useful site for Web searches that lets you collect, compare and share information on one page. The site started out as a way to do comparison shopping but the site's technology can be used to collect and share information and get feedback from others on virtually any topic such as vacations or creating gift registries. Kaboodle, Inc., www.kaboodle.com

TagWorld lets you share your photos, videos, blogs, bookmarks and more. TagWorld, www.tagworld.com

Yahoo! My Web 2.0 lets you save and share bookmarks and discover new Web pages through the online community. Yahoo! Inc., http://myweb2.search.yahoo.com

Computer Help

If you're looking for ways to solve your computer problems, try these sites.

Product Tips: Computer Help Sites

Answers That Work helps you troubleshoot and find answers to your computing problems and issues. www.answersthatwork.com

Experts Exchange provides access to IT professionals to promote collaboration and sharing. Exchange LLC, www.experts-exchange.com

GRC.com has been offering a potpourri of quality computer solutions and information for years. Gibson Research Corp., www.grc.com

PC Mechanic is a plain-English website with do-it-yourself information on personal computers. The site hosts a wide variety of tutorials, editorials, weekly columns and reviews. PC Media, Inc., www.pcmech.com

Computer Security Information

With computer security issues now common front page stories, it pays to stay up to date on security issues and solutions.

Product Tips: Computer Security Sites

CERT Coordination Center (CERT/CC) is a center of Internet security expertise. This is a good place to stay up to date on security issues and information. www.cert.org

Identity Theft Resource Center has tips, resources and alerts for victims and people who want to avoid becoming victims. www.idtheftcenter.org

Spyware Warrior is a website with tips and articles on spyware and antispyware, a forum to discuss spyware issues and solutions and much more. www.spywarewarrior.com

StopBadWare is an initiative launched by Harvard University and the Oxford Internet Institute against spyware and other malicious software programs with the goal of becoming a central clearinghouse for research and fighting malware programs. www.stopbadware.org

Consumer Shopping Research

Money isn't everything…but there's no sense overpaying on a purchase. Maybe more important than paying the right price is making sure you're buying the right item. There are websites devoted just to prices, reviews, complaints or a combination.

To distinguish themselves, some sites are including protection against buying from fraudulent vendors and/or are providing warnings about possible phishing sites. These research and comparison sites will be leapfrogging each other by adding benefits in a race to attract your business.

Product Tips: Shopping Research/Price Comparison Sites

Become.com is a shopping research and price comparison service that includes buying guides, consumer reviews, articles, specifications, forums and comparison pricing information. Over seven million products are available. You'll also see searches other Become users have performed, real-time suggestions from the site on search terms you may want to use and news (and links) from top U.S. news sources related to your shopping. Become, Inc., www.become.com

Bizrate.com is a shopping search site that uses price, popularity, product availability and merchant reputation for its ranking system. Their index includes over 30 million products from more than 40,000 stores. Shopzilla, Inc., www.bizrate.com

Buysafeshopping.com offers more than two million items including listings from eBay and Overstock.com auctions.

Using surety bonds from Liberty Mutual, at this time buySAFE also guarantees every transaction up to $25,000. buySAFE, Inc., www.buysafeshopping.com

Complaints.com airs consumer grievances. You might want to check it out before you make your next purchase. Sagacity Corp., www.complaints.com

Froogle is Google's shopping search engine. Google, Inc., http://froogle.google.com

MyRatePlan.com lets you compare cellphone plans to find what's best for you and/or your family. MyRatePlan.com, LLC, www.MyRatePlan.com

MySimon is a well-known shopping search engine. CNET Networks, Inc., www.mysimon.com

PriceGrabber.com offers price comparisons, product reviews and side-by-side product comparisons. Pricegrabber.com, LLC, www.pricegrabber.com

PriceRunner is a top-rated price guide and shopping comparison site. Pricerunner, www.pricerunner.com

PriceWatch is street price search engine for computer components and peripherals. www.pricewatch.com

Shopping.com has millions of products, thousands of merchants and millions of reviews from the Epinions community. eBay, Inc., www.shopping.com

Product Tips: Coupon Sites

It may also pay to look for coupon sites.

CouponMountain, Mezi Media, www.couponmountain.com

Fatwallet, FatWallet, Inc., www.fatwallet.com

GottaDeal, OlsenNet LLC, www.gottadeal.com

Product Tip: Real Estate Valuation Site

Zillow.com gives you its "zestimate" of real estate values for properties in its database. It's being beta-tested as this book is being written. Zillow, www.zillow.com

Finding a Job

Looking for a job isn't fun and it's time consuming. Below are some sites to make the process a bit easier.

Product Tips: Job Finders

America's Career Info Net is a one-step career and job center sponsored by the government. www.acinet.org

Indeed.com is a search engine for jobs that includes job listings from thousands of websites—major job boards, newspapers, associations and company career pages. Indeed, Inc., www.indeed.com

Jobster Search is a metasearch engine for jobs. Jobster, Inc., www.jobster.com

Monster is a well-known job search site. Monster Worldwide, Inc., www.monster.com

Simply Hired is a vertical search engine company whose goal is to build the largest online database of jobs on the planet. Simply Hired, Inc., www.simplyhired.com

Identity Theft Warning for Job Seekers

Be careful in posting resumes and responding to online job offers. Some identity thieves are emailing "job application" and "background check" forms as a way to get your personal information.

Maps

Maps combined with search services (e.g., restaurants or real estate services) are one of the fastest growing areas of the Web. *Mashups* combine online maps with lists of data to show specific locations of jobs, rentals, real estate listings, and, in time, probably nearly every bit of information. With *3D Situational Awareness* technology, aerial photographs are combined with ground level pictures or video.

Windows Live Local (http://local.live.com) gives you a 45-degree bird's eye view of certain major U.S. cities combined with local search, driving directions and Yellow Page tools. The site is being beta-tested as this book is being written.

The *Google Maps Webcam Locator* lets you do virtual sightseeing and even see the weather live. For links to webcams around the world, go to http://www.google.com/alpha/Top/Computers/Internet/On_the_Web/Webcams/Directories/

One of the coolest "travel" sites is earth.google.com which lets you travel virtually to famous sites around the world or just to the places where you grew up to show your kids or yourself how those child-hood memories have changed in reality over the years. http://earth.google.com

News, Groups and More

No matter who or what you want to find, there's probably a site out there to help you.

Product Tips: Databases and More

Bloglines is a free online service that helps you subscribe to and manage Web information such as news feeds, weblogs and audio. IAC Search & Media, www.bloglines.com

Daypop searches 59,000 news sites plus weblogs and RSS feeds. Daypop, www.daypop.com

Firstgov.gov is the official website of the federal government. www.firstgov.gov

Google Groups helps you locate information in Usenet communities. Google, Inc., www.groups.google.com

Podcasting

Podcasting comes from combining the words *iPod* and *broadcasting*. *Podcasts* are audio and video programs delivered over the Internet or other means and are played on iPods, other portable players and computers. You don't need to have an iPod to hear podcasted programs. Any computer or digital audio (or video) player can play podcasts. Podcasts can also be delivered to cellphones and this is known as *clipcasting*.

What is different about podcasting is its method of delivery. It uses feeds such as RSS feeds to deliver the audio content through subscriptions. *Podcatching* or *aggregator software* can automatically push new content to your device once you subscribe.

Product Tip: Podcasting Info and How-To's

PodCast411.com can provide you with a directory of podcasts, teach you how to get podcasts or show you how to podcast yourself. www.PodCast411.com

With podcasts growing in number and popularity, sites are developing tools to help you find, rate, organize and download podcasts. (Unfortunately, with spam now hitting blogs (*splogs*), it's probably just a matter of time before you will also have to deal with *spamcasts* —spam affecting podcasts.)

Product Tips: Podcast Search and Organizing Sites

Here's a sampling of the available sites:

Allpodcasts.com, OpinionatedGreek, Ltd., www.allpodcasts.com

Digitalpodcast.com, Bella Ventures, Inc., www.digitalpodcast.com

Odeo.com, Odeo, Inc., www.odeo.com

Podcastalley.com, Podcastalley, www.podcastalley.com

Podcastbunker.com, Podcast Bunker,
www.podcastbunker.com

Podcast.net, Podcast Networks, www.podcast.net

Podzinger.com is a podcast search engine that lets you search the full audio of podcasts just like you search for any other information on the Web. The search results include snippets from the audio to help you determine whether the results are relevant. You can also click on the broadcasted words to listen to the audio from that point. BBN Technologies Corp., www.podzinger.com

Singingfish.com, Singingfish, www.singingfish.com

Product Tip: Video Sharing

Bliptv is a video blogging, podcasting and sharing service. It is being beta-tested as this book is being written. Bliptv, www.blip.tv

See the hearing health warning in Chapter 16 on MP3 players.

Travel Search Tools

Here are some of the best travel sites.

Product Tips: Travel Sites

Expedia lets you research, plan and book your travel needs. Expedia, Inc., www.expedia.com

FAA (Federal Aviation Administration) issues the federal rules on the maximum size bag for airlines. But you'll want to check with each airline you use (or *SeatGuru.com* below) to see what their specific guidelines are for carry-on luggage; in certain situations an airline may require most or even all of your bags to be checked. There can be some variation in guidelines by different airlines, depending on factors such as aircraft size and the number of passengers on a flight. www.faa.gov/passengers

Google Maps offers free directions, maps and satellite views. Google, Inc., www.maps.google.com

Kayak is a metasearch tool that searches many sites at once to find travel costs and options for flights, hotels and cars. Kayak.com, www.kayak.com

Magellan's is a leading source of travel supplies. Magellan's Travel Supplies, www.magellans.com

Mapquest.com provides excellent free directions and maps. MapQuest, Inc., www.mapquest.com

Moment's Notice is a *short-notice* discount travel club that acts as a clearinghouse for the travel industry's unsold space. Substantial discounts apply to cruises, tours and flights. Moment's Notice, www.moments-notice.com

No-smoke.org helps you find smoke-free rooms. Click *Smokefree Travel* on the website. www.no-smoke.org

OAG is a global content management company providing a broad range of travel and transport products for business and consumer customers accessible through the Internet, on mobile devices or in print. For business travelers, OAG has several products for planning and making travel arrangements. OAG is best known for its database of airline schedules which includes flight details for 1,000 airlines and more than 3,000 airports. The database is updated approximately ten times every second. This flight database can be critically important, for example, if your flight is unexpectedly cancelled and you need to find another one right away on another airline. OAG, www.oag.com

Orbitz is a search engine for finding deals on airfare, lodging, car rentals, cruises, vacation packages and other travel. Orbitz also monitors nationwide travel conditions around the clock and gathers and interprets FAA, National Weather Service and other data for its travelers. Orbitz, LLC, www.orbitz.com

SeatGuru provides information on airplane seat sizes, legroom and location (window or aisle); baggage; check-in; traveling with infants or pets; Unaccompanied Minor service; and in-flight amenities and services such as laptop power, audio/video entertainment and food and beverage service.
SeatGuru.com, Inc., www.seatguru.com

Smarter Travel gives you discounted last-minute air fares that are easily searchable. Smarter Living, Inc., www.smartertravel.com

The Travel Insider website has articles, a free weekly newsletter and other information on travel-related topics designed to save you money or substantially improve the quality of your travel experiences in non-cash ways.
The Travel Insider LLC, www.travelinsider.info

Travelocity is a well-known online travel booking agency. Travelocity LP, www.travelocity.com

TripAdvisor.com is a travel experience wiki (a wiki is similar to an online bulletin board) where fellow travelers share their experiences. www.TripAdvisor.com

WikiTravel.org is another travel experience wiki. www.WikiTravel.org

Frequent Hotel-Guest Phishing Warning

It just never stops. Some *super-platinum* or other *frequent guest* members are receiving email offers for a chance to win a free hotel stay by clicking on a link to what appears to be the hotel's website. It isn't the hotel site. It's a scam to get you to enter your hotel club account number and password on the phony site which is later used by the phisher to get your personal information that's in your hotel frequent guest account.

Sometimes your searches are closer to home rather than around the globe on the World Wide Web. That's why you'll want to read Part 4 to see how to search, organize and back up your computer.

Part 4
Dancing Cheek-to-Cheek

Managing Your Computer and Your Info

11

Organizing and Finding Your Files, Notes and Other Digital Info

Sometimes we romanticize about how good things were in the good old days—the music, the dancing…but not the computers. In 1984, we bought our first computers and Don got a second internal hard disk for his computer. That extra 10 MB (megabytes, not gigabytes) hard drive cost $800.

Since then hard drive storage capacity in general has increased by more than 5,000,000% but prices have plummeted. Thank goodness hard drive prices have gone down since Don bought that 10 MB drive back in 1984. Otherwise, a 500 GB (gigabyte) drive bought today at the 1984 price per megabyte would cost $40 million. So much for the good old days.

In the next five years, hard disk drives are expected to increase *at least* ten-fold in size. Gigabyte drives will join megabyte drives as dinosaurs and terabyte hard drives will be the next measuring stick. But that won't be the end of it. Future holographic drives with 3D images will dwarf today's drives in size and speed and the ability to pack realism onto a computer screen.

As hard disks continue to get larger in capacity, it will be more important than ever to keep your files and folders organized and up to date.

When it comes to the data on your computer, you want to be able to

- Organize and find it (discussed in this chapter and in Chapter 12)

- Back it up (Chapter 13)

- Protect it (Chapters 1 through 3)

In this chapter we'll explore the following software programs to help you organize and find the bits, bytes and pieces of information on your computer's hard disk:

1. Desktop search programs that use keywords to find a file or email

2. Note taking and organizing software to help find *and* organize your information

3. PIMs (personal information managers) and other contact manager programs that give you ways to control your calendar and keep track of your contacts, scheduled activities, messages and calls

4. Photo organizing and sharing programs

Desktop Search Programs

If your files aren't as organized as you'd like them to be, a desktop search program may help you find that needle in a haystack. And with the size of hard drives these days, it may be more like finding a needle in a silo. These programs continue to evolve by adding new features and benefits.

Tip: One is Plenty

If you decide to use this type of program, get only one of them since multiple programs in this genre can not only slow down computer performance but also interfere with one another.

Warning: Not a Replacement for Organized Folders

Although finding individual files has gotten very quick and easy with desktop search programs, neglecting computer organization and housekeeping means (a) it will be difficult to find *related* files in one place on your computer; (b) your computer will work harder and run slower; and (c) backing up your files will take more time.

Privacy Warning

Not only do these programs make it quick for you to search for information on your computer, they can do the same for anyone else who gets hold of your computer (in person or over the Internet), even for a little bit of time.

Because these search programs are instant finding programs, a search on your computer, for example, for "Social Security Number" could quickly turn up every place it appears on your computer's hard disk.

To help prevent problems, have password protection or more sophisticated authentication procedures in place to operate your computer.

Also, if you're using one of the second-generation desktop search programs that can also search across multiple computers, you might want to keep this multi-computer search feature turned off entirely or at least specify that certain sensitive files, folders, emails and/or your Web searching history not be shared among the computers. If you decide to use the multiple computer search feature, the desktop search program company may copy and store your data (for a limited or possibly an indefinite period of time) on the search engine's servers. Whenever a copy of your data is in the hands of someone else for any period of time, the chances of that data being used, released or subpoenaed go up.

One Dozen Desktop Search Program Features

The desktop search programs are not identical in what they do or how they do it.

As with many other areas of the computer world, you can't go by what something is called to know all that it does. For example, Google has a widget-type feature called *Sidebar* in its desktop search tool. *Sidebar* is software that brings information such as the news, weather, stock quotes, syndicated website feeds, photos and other personalized information to your desktop without your having to open a Web browser. Sidebar also lets you share content via email or IM (as a collaboration or sharing tool). Google, Inc., www.google.com

Here are one dozen features to look for in a desktop search program:

1. The ability to restrict others from using this program on your computer

Tip: Keeping Your Privacy

You may want to restrict *not only* outsiders from seeing your data but also the people who *share* your computer. For Windows users, for example, it may be that there are privacy options to encrypt the index only if users have separate Windows accounts with different usernames to log on. However, if users share the same Windows account on a single computer, then any user might be able to search all indexed activity on that computer. Check this out before adding a desktop search program. You may also be able to limit access to specified folders, files, email folders and your Web searching history preferably by excluding items *before* an index is created so you don't have to manually delete them from the index.

2. Whether it supports the Internet browsers and email programs you use

3. Indexing both the subject and content of emails (including deleted emails you may not want indexed) — check the preferences setting on a program

4. Indexing the content of email attachments as well as the attachment name

5. Indexing instant messages, calendars and contact information

6. Indexing all the files you regularly use (e.g., Word, PowerPoint, PDF, HTML files)

7. Indexing Zip files by content and name

8. The length of time to initially index and then to keep the index up to date

> ### Tip: Indexing and Performance Speed
> To keep the index up to date, some programs need the search feature turned on all the time to avoid doing a complete and time-consuming reindexing of all information. Unless a program does this in the background when your computer is otherwise idle, it may slow down performance. (However, more powerful computers such as those with dual-core chips shouldn't be slowed down — see Chapter 17.) Other programs do the indexing at scheduled nonpeak times when you're not using the computer for your work. Read current reviews in leading computer magazines (such as *PC Magazine* or *PC World*) to see how the indexing speed of the programs is rated.

9. Whether it searches all your data *at one time* (e.g., your files *and* your email or your files *and* a Web-based search) or in separate searches — the fewer searches you need to do, the better

10. The search methods available (whole words, partial words, phrases, Boolean searches, names of document authors, dates of documents) — the more ways you have to search, the better

11. How search results are shown (thumbnails, excerpts, whole files) — it's always nice to have the option of seeing whole files to get a better context for the search results

12. Whether searched files can be launched from the search program to avoid having to load up the application (e.g., a word processing program)

Here are three leading desktop search programs. They will continue to add features to match and outdo one another so be on the lookout for continuing changes, especially in security features.

Product Tips: Desktop Search Programs

Copernic Desktop Search is an easy-to-use search engine that lets you instantly search files, emails and email attachments stored anywhere on your computer's hard drive. It executes sub-second searching of Microsoft Word, Excel and PowerPoint files, Acrobat PDFs and popular music, picture and video formats. It can also search your browser history, favorites and contacts. As you add more terms to your search request, search results are narrowed down right before your eyes. As you scroll through the results, previews of the files or emails are shown on the bottom of the screen. Click *open* and the file or email opens using its native application. Copernic Technologies Inc., www. copernic.com

Google Desktop searches your computer (or multiple computers) and the Web. It provides a full text search of your emails, computer files, music, photos, chats and Web pages that you've viewed. Google, Inc., www.google.com

X1 is a fast program to search for a particular file, email or other information on your computer's hard disk. As you type in characters, words or phrases, the search results are displayed and refined. With its over 370 built-in file viewers for the most common file formats including Word documents, spreadsheets, databases, presentations, PDFs, graphics and more, you can view files even if you don't have the original software applications that created the files. To increase your productivity, the program can also do typical commands (e.g., reply to email) without your having to leave the program and open up the original application. The program allows you to choose either continual indexing (to always have updated information) or to have indexing done in the background or at scheduled times (which avoids interference with your computer's performance). X1 Technologies, Inc., www.x1.com

Alternative File and Information Management Tools

A Task-Based File System

Here's a unique tool for organizing and accessing your files including your emails.

Product Tip: Information Manager with Integrated Email and File Management

EverDesk uniquely integrates email and file management. You can manage emails side by side with the rest of your files in Windows folders so related emails, attachments and other files (including documents, links and contacts) can be grouped and managed together in a centralized location. By providing a unified system for managing emails and files, EverDesk makes it possible for you to organize relevant information across *tasks* rather than applications. EverDesk also provides enhanced flexibility in working with email attachments, multimedia previewing capability for a wide variety of files and integrated encryption. EverEZ Systems Ltd., www.everdesk.com

Virtual File Folders

When you organize information in your brain, you don't always group or categorize a piece of information in just one way. There may be many different thoughts that come to mind when you're thinking of someone or something. That's where *virtual folders* come in.

They let you link, reorganize and view files *virtually* (regardless of their actual location on your computer and without having to move them) according to attributes such as the document author's name, date of file creation or various keywords.

If you're using a Macintosh, you already have access to virtual file folders. Windows Vista, the successor to Windows XP, should have a similar capability. The Spotlight feature in the Mac's Tiger operating system lets you find files, emails, contacts, calendars and even images in a matter of seconds and takes the searching capability a step further by letting you set up virtual folders called Smart Folders.

How Mac Smart Folders Work

You can take search results and save them as a Smart Folder that automatically updates as you add or remove documents from your Mac. Smart Folders contain files grouped together in virtual folders based on search criteria instead of physical location. That way the same file can appear in multiple Smart Folders without moving it from its original saved location on your system. The software keeps it organized for you without the need to duplicate or shift files. Apple Computer, Inc., www.apple.com

Finding Your Notes and Other Information

If you want a software program to store, organize and find your notes, another type of software may be useful for you.

Product Tips: Note Taking and Organizing Software and Websites

askSam is a highly-rated free-form database that combines database, text-retrieval and word processing functions to manage both structured and free-form information. You can import information from a variety of sources including email and online research and communications. You can easily search for any word or phrase and generate database reports. You can share and distribute information using the network and electronic publishing versions. askSam Systems, 800/800-1997 [FL] or www.asksam.com

BackPack is a website that lets you write down notes, ideas or to-do lists and then have reminders sent to you via email or a phone call. BackPack also lets you organize events, collaborate and more. 37signals LLC, www.backpackit.com

EverNote gives you one place to capture, store and find your typed and handwritten notes, memos, emails, phone messages, documents and Web pages. (This is more than a search utility—it's a separate application.) The "notes" are stored on one endless, virtual roll of paper rather than saving information in a new file for each bit of information. You can clip Web content, drag-and-drop text or images or type in text. To keep you even more organized, when you copy content, the program keeps track of the source of the material and lets you refer back to see the original source whether it's a document, email or Web page. You can find notes in several ways including keywords, categories you set up or those that are automatically assigned when you create a note. You can create multiple categories for the same information so you're not restricted to labeling or filing it one way. EverNote Corp., www.evernote.com

Info Select is a fast way to deal with notes, ideas, plans, contacts and all your random information. It's a personal information manager that is a free-form text database that lets you make miscellaneous notes on computer (instead of on paper slips) and search for them instantaneously. If you keep a lot of miscellaneous notes or ideas that are unrelated to each other or to particular projects or people, this could be a handy program. Info Select can be used for managing email and NNTP news, Web pages, images, contacts, calendar events and files stored on your hard drive. Micro Logic Corp., 201/447-6991 [NJ] or www.miclog.com

Microsoft OneNote lets you take notes on your computer and arrange pages into tabbed sections by topic. OneNote gives you one place for all your notes and the freedom to organize them the way you want. It also helps you capture information in multiple ways and then organize and reuse that information according to your needs. OneNote will be renamed as Office OneNote 2007 in the next version of Microsoft Office, Office 2007. Microsoft Corp., www.microsoft.com

Calendars and Contacts

Web-Based Calendars

Web-based calendars are a good example of how Web-based solutions can work for you to organize, coordinate and access scheduling information.

Online calendars are increasing in popularity for three reasons:

1. You can always have your calendar with you if you have an Internet connection.

2. You can have one calendar to consolidate all of your items.

3. An online calendar gives coworkers and project team members access for scheduling meetings and calls and for coordinating work assignments.

You can usually allow or restrict access to your online calendar or just parts of it. For example, you could allow access to your business calendar but not your personal calendar.

Product Tips: Online Calendars and Organizers

There's no shortage of free online calendars. Web portals offer online calendars. Some Internet service providers (ISPs) and websites also provide free online organizers or PIM (personal information manager) services. You may want a more complete, fee-based online solution such as the following online calendar:

OneCalendar is a connected Web-based calendar that you

can use to bring your work, personal, family and community group calendars together into one easy-to-use online calendar. OneCalendar enables you to share calendars with individuals or groups by posting calendars on the Web or emailing the calendar using built-in tools. You can even organize your combined multiple calendars in a color-coded list.
Trumba Corp., www.trumba.com

PIMs and Other Contact Manager Programs

You may want a specialized software program to help you organize and find all of your business and personal contacts on your computer or mobile device. If you need more than a computerized address book, that's where easy-to-use PIMs and other contact management programs come in.

This database-type software goes under many names: contact manager, PIM (personal information manager) or CRM (customer relationship management) software.

This type of software can help you:

1. Store and find names, addresses and phone numbers

2. Stay in contact with a large number of people

3. Schedule and track calls and meetings

4. Have reminders with alarms on follow-up calls

5. Provide a way to take and retrieve notes on your contacts

6. Sort, search and report information

7. Print mailing labels

8. Do mail merges using your own word processor or a built-in word processor that prints form letters

In addition, many of these programs come with strong workgroup capabilities so you can easily manage personal and group calendars and schedules on and off the Web.

Product Tips: Contact Manager Software

ACT! by Sage is a powerful, award-winning, easy-to-use contact and customer management program designed for sales professionals, small teams, corporate workgroups and mobile professionals. It offers a tightly integrated contact database, word processor, report generator, an activities scheduler and sales opportunity tracking tools. It's available in two versions: ACT! by Sage is for individuals and small teams of up to 10 networked users and *ACT! by Sage Premium for Workgroups* is for workgroups of up to 50 networked users. These ACT! programs each include *ACT! Link for Palm OS* and *ACT! Link for Pocket PC* to synchronize ACT! data (including contacts, notes, history, appointments, activities, to-do's and custom data fields) with handheld devices. Sage Software, 877/501-4496 [CA] or www.act.com

GoldMine is a comprehensive contact manager for networks and remote users. This powerful enterprise-wide business tool lets you automate common repetitive office tasks with its "Automated Processes." Features include calendaring, email, mail merge letters, telemarketing, sales forecasting, lead tracking, fax/merge, wireless data synchronization, communication server capability, sophisticated security, "remote transfer synchronization," report generator, user definable screens and fields and unlimited additional contacts. FrontRange Solutions, Inc., 800/776-7889 ext 7378 [CA] or www.goldmine.com

Microsoft Access is an easy-to-use, fast relational database management system that's good for beginners, experienced users and even developers. Workgroup features enable you to share information with others with or without intranets. Microsoft Corp., www.microsoft.com

Web-Based Contact Data

With data on clients or customers located on the Web, you can get real-time information from virtually anywhere and not have to deal with synchronization issues.

Product Tips: Web-Based Access to Your Contacts and Data

ACT! by Sage Premium for Web delivers anytime, any-where access to centralized data. This enables remote, traveling or on-site users to access information in real time through a Web browser. This program works as a standalone product or in conjunction with *ACT! Sage Premium for Workgroups*. Sage Software, 877/501-4496 [CA] or www.act.com

iGoldMine gives you real-time access to all of your cus-tomer and prospect information. You can view contacts and calendars, communicate via email and use auto-mated processes and other GoldMine features. Its real-time access replaces synchronization with live, remote access to information. FrontRange Solutions, 800/776-7889 [CA] or www.goldmine.com

Web-Based Downsides

Before you go with an online approach, consider these four issues:

1. Accessing the Web may not be fast enough depending on the speed of your Internet connection.

2. Your Internet connection may go down sometimes and be unavail-able.

3. It may be much more convenient to just have all of this information on your computer or mobile device so the information is already at your fingertips.

4. Security and privacy issues are more problematic when you deal with the Web.

Finding Your Photos

More and more, we're saving large numbers of images on our com-puters and external hard drives. Without the right software, it can be difficult to organize and locate photos and images. The right program can help you see the big picture and all the little ones, too.

Product Tips: Photo Organizing and Editing Programs

Adobe Photoshop Album helps you organize and touch up digital pictures. Adobe, Inc., www.adobe.com

Memory Manager software helps you easily create and share digital photo albums using journaling and scrapbooking techniques. Creative Memories, 800/468-9335 [MN] or www.creativememories.com

Picasa is a free, award-winning photo organizing, editing and sharing program. *Picasa's Hello* is an instant messenger photo-sharing program. Google, Inc., www.picasa.com

Online Storage Warning

Online storage services are not all alike. Under the terms and conditions of some online vendors, your online photos, other images and information could be destroyed by the online service or become inaccessible to you. Read the fine print before you sign up for online storage arrangements, especially free and/or unlimited storage arrangements. In some cases, for example, your photos may be deleted by the online storage vendor if you don't purchase a minimum amount of services or log in and view your images within a specified period of time (e.g., every 90 days). At the time this book is being writen, in the case of Yahoo!, if you die, no one has access to your photos stored online (see the *No Right of Survivorship and Non-Transferability* paragraph in the Yahoo! Terms of Service). And if an online provider goes bankrupt, you may lose access, too.

Despite all the alternative ways you have to access your info, you still need to take advantage of the built-in file management system on your computer's operating system. We'll tell you how and why in Chapter 12.

12

Organizing
Your
Computer

Just as there are key steps in dancing, there are key steps to organizing your computer.

Before desktop search programs came into the picture, it was essential to organize your computer to find files. Now the need to organize is partially for finding related files but more so for helping you back up your computer and speeding up computer performance.

With hard disks getting bigger and containing maybe hundreds of thousands of files, it's important to minimize how many of those files you must back up each time so the backup process doesn't take too long to complete.

The quicker the backup process is completed, the more likely you are to back up regularly. And with computer crashes and computer viruses that can poison your files an ever-constant threat, it's vital that you maintain current backups.

To speed up the backup process, start with an organized computer, which in turn begins with three important steps.

Step 1: Partition Your Computer's Hard Disk to Divide and Conquer

The first step is *partitioning* (separating) your computer's hard disk into two or more *partitions* (sections) so you can separate files for backups.

By partitioning the contents of your computer's hard disk, you're organizing the contents into broad categories. Partition one section to hold your computer's operating system (e.g., Windows), software applications and programs. Partition another section for the documents you create such as word processing documents, spreadsheets and presentations as well as files such as videos, photos and music. As discussed later in this chapter, you may want to create a third partition for your large video files.

You partition your computer's hard disk with partitioning software. Although we've been using partitioning software for a long time without any problems, we remember that it was scary the first time we used it. The thought of making a major change to a hard drive on a computer and rearranging the data on it gave us great motivation to have a complete and current backup before venturing into this new territory.

Product Tip: Partitioning Software

Partition Magic is an award-winning partitioning software program designed to let you organize your hard drive by creating, resizing, moving, splitting, copying, merging and converting disk partitions quickly and easily while protecting the integrity of your data. Symantec, www.symantec.com

The Benefits of Partitioning

Partitions allow you to separate your data and files (what you create) from your computer's operating system and your software programs. Separating them this way makes it much easier and faster to do backups since usually it's just your data files that you need to put on a more frequent backup routine. They're the files that are most likely to change from day to day, week to week. If you're also backing up your operating system and all of your software programs with every backup, that's a needless time drain.

How Partitioning Works

The hard disk in your computer is automatically designated as your "C drive" by the manufacturer and the operating system software. When you partition a hard disk, the C drive is divided up into partitions such as the C partition and the D partition. The partitions would be located on the one actual, *physical* hard drive (the C drive).

On the C partition, you could put your operating system and your other software. On the D partition, you could have all of the data files you create (including the My Documents folder) that need to be backed up more frequently. For your more regular backups, you would just back up the D partition. Also, by having your data files in a separate place, it makes them more organized and easier to visually locate.

Step 2: Set Up Your Computer Folder System

Once you've organized the hard disk into partitions, you're ready to take advantage of your computer's built-in folder system. This system lets you create logical categories (called folders) and subcategories (called subfolders) to place all the contents (files) on your computer's hard disk. Rather than throw everything together, it's better to place related files in the same folder or subfolders.

The term *files* includes but isn't limited to word processing documents, spreadsheets, presentations, images, applications, Web pages, audio/video files and databases. Computer *folders* can hold files as well as other folders and are a great organizing tool.

Tip: Benefits of Using a Folder System

Even if you're using a desktop search program, it still pays for you to organize your files and folders logically for backup purposes and to quickly spot related or similar files and folders, say through Windows Explorer.

Tip: Have Distinctive Folder Icons

If you want to spot certain folders more quickly in Windows Explorer, customize those folder icons. Here are the steps: (1) right click on a folder while you're in Windows Explorer, (2) left click *Properties*, (3) left click *Customize*, (4) left click *Change Icon*, (5) review the icon possibilities and select one by left clicking on it, (6) left click *OK* and (7) left click *OK* again. Now your new icon should appear to the left on the folder name and be easier to spot.

Eight Guidelines

Keep your system as simple and as accessible as possible by following these eight guidelines:

1. **Make your paper and computer file management systems consistent with one another whenever feasible.**
   Try to use similar naming conventions if possible especially if you share files with other people.

2. **Keep the folders you use most often, the most accessible.**
   An accessible place is the My Documents section of your computer's hard disk. (My Documents is expected to be renamed as "Documents" in Windows Vista, the successor to Windows XP).

3. **Be consistent and brief rather than creative in coming up with names for folders, subfolders and files.**
   But don't make names so short you can't tell what they mean at a quick glance.

4. **Have your folder and subfolder names parallel one another.**
   For example, if you have consulting clients, each client might get their own folder by their last name with subfolders for Proposals, Letters, Invoices and Reports. A good way of looking at it is whether a spouse or fellow employee could easily make sense of your naming method — unless, of course, you wouldn't want your spouse or a fellow employee to understand how your computer is organized.

5. **Limit the number of files you keep in each folder.**
   The fewer files you have in a folder, the faster it is to find them — especially the files you use most often and any related files.

6. **Limit the number of levels of subfolders.**
   In general, you don't want to go more than three levels deep.

7. **Consolidate your files.**
   For example, instead of having every letter to a client in many separate files, group all the year 2007 letters to a client together in one document file. This can not only save space on your computer but make it easier to locate the letters.

8. **Have separate folders for each person's data.**
   If you share your computer with other people, have separate folders for each person's data.

Step 3: Spring Clean Your Computer's Hard Disk

There's a good reason to do regular computer housekeeping, especially computer file maintenance. It will improve the speed of your computer — particularly the hard disk — and it will help you work more efficiently, too.

File Maintenance

Your computer's operating system comes with a built-in basic file management program to find, save, copy, move and delete files and perform housekeeping and preventative maintenance chores on the computer's hard disk.

There are also specialized, third-party programs with greater or different capabilities that work with or separately from your usual file management program.

These programs help you eliminate duplicate and unneeded files as well as transfer and consolidate files.

Product Tip: File Management Program

Directory Opus offers a complete replacement for Windows Explorer. You can create virtual folders where you group files from different locations in a collection to view and interact with them as if they were all in the same folder. You can search a folder or hard drive for duplicate files. The program's multi-threaded design lets you perform multiple operations simultaneously. At the same time, you can download files from a website, zip files into one folder, unzip files into another and copy yet more files between your local folders. GP Software, www.gpsoft.com.au

Defragment (Optimize) Your Computer's Hard Disk

After eliminating, transferring, organizing and consolidating files, your computer may appear neat and tidy, but chances are that many of the remaining files were and probably still are *fragmented*. Fragmented files have a file's information scattered in different places over your computer's hard disk.

When you save a file to a disk, the disk looks for the first available free space. If only part of a file fits there, that's where the first part goes. Then your disk looks for other places to store the balance of a file. As a result, the more you use your computer's hard disk, the slower it becomes because information for any one file may be scattered as *fragments* in many places on the hard disk. The more scattered the stored information, the longer it takes for your computer to pull all the pieces together so you can work with a file. Also, disk fragmentation can cause crashes, slowdowns, freeze-ups and even total system failures.

The way to fix this and speed up your computer is to *defragment* (or *optimize*) your disk by using either the computer operating system's built-in disk defragmenter or a separate defragging program. It's a good idea to check once or twice a month to see if your disk needs to be defragmented. We'd suggest backing up your computer before you defrag it since your hard drive's contents are being moved around and rearranged by the optimizing.

Product Tips: Disk Defragmenting Programs

Diskeeper is a top-rated program that improves your computer's performance by defragging your files. It offers a Set It and Forget It mode to automate the process. Diskeeper Corp., www.diskeeper.com

PerfectDisk is another top defragging utility program. Raxco Software, Inc., 800/546-9728 [MD] or www.raxco.com

Once your computer's organized, you're ready to do an up-to-date backup. We can't remember when we were ever sorry we had a current backup on hand.

13

Backing Up Your Computer

When you cross a dance floor to ask someone to dance, you hope the answer will be "yes." But life sometimes throws you some curve balls. That's why it's a good idea to have a backup plan in place whether you strike out on or off the dance floor.

Backup Warning

As writer Wes Nihei observed in *PC World*, "Backing up files is a lot like dental hygiene: by the time you get serious about flossing and brushing, it's usually too late." Or as Wally Beddoe put it, "There are basically two types of computer users: those who have lost data and those who will."

Remember that first computer of Don's in 1984 with the two 10 MB internal hard drives? Don won't forget the first time he ran a disk diagnosis and repair program for no particular reason other than to see whether the hard drives had any problems. Well, the diagnosis program had a bug in it and the bug accidentally destroyed all of his data on both drives. He would have jumped out the window except for two things—his office was on the first floor and he had recently made a backup of both hard drives. That's when we both learned about the importance of backups.

Backups are cheap insurance policies for disasters *before* they strike.

Why Should You Back Up?

You never backed up your filing cabinets; why should you back up your computer files?

1. The chances of losing all your computer data are much greater than losing your hard data.

2. More of our lives are digital—our photos, emails, finances and essential documents.

3. If you're using a laptop computer or USB thumb drive, it may be stolen or you may lose it.

4. Physical disasters can strike at any time and with great intensity.

5. It's so easy today to back up.

6. Viruses and other malware may infect your computer and your files.

Virus and Reformatting Warning

Sometimes the only way to remove computer viruses and other malware is to give your computer a complete clean start by reformatting your computer's hard disk and *wiping out everything* on it. That's when you'll be so glad you have a good, clean backup to reinstall on your computer.

Backup Basics

Your computer backup plan should be to have a duplicate copy of computer data—the files you create as well as the software programs and operating system on your computer—stored somewhere else. For important information, make two backups and keep one off-site—for example, one at home and one at the office (or one copy online).

Although you could store a backup on another partition of your computer's hard drive, you're better off having a backup on another device (e.g., an external hard drive) or stored online. In time, you'll see *NAS* (*network-attached storage*) used with more home networks.

Good computer backups let you conduct business as usual even if your computer's hard disk crashes, a virus poisons your files or your computer is in for repair. Don't wait until a crash to get serious about backing up. Backups are insurance for your valuable, current data (which would either require more than 15 minutes to redo or would be next to impossible to recreate); your long-term files and records; and your software programs.

Personal Backup Tip

Whenever we're producing original, creative material, we save it at least twice—once on a hard disk and also on a USB thumb drive. Then we periodically also back it up on an external hard drive and/or online.

Quick Big Picture Backup Advice

Our backup advice is: (1) buy a large external hard disk for major backups, (2) get a USB drive that's at least 1 GB for daily backups of changed files, (3) purchase backup software such as *Retrospect* by EMC Corp., (4) set up a daily (or hourly) backup routine for changed files and a weekly, monthly or no more than quarterly schedule for major, complete backups and (5) have at least two sets of backups with one set kept off-site.

Backup and Encryption

Since it's no longer unusual to hear about off-site thefts of backed up data, encryption is becoming a more standard part of backups.

Use Rollback Software
to Get a Do-Over

Of course, you always want to have at least one good backup available. But when it comes to problems with your computer, you always want to have extra options. That's why before we get into more traditional backup programs, media and routines, see how rollback software may be your computer mulligan, that extra option for a do-over that you'll need someday.

What would you do if you needed a recent or good backup but you didn't have one? There are two ways you may be able to get a second chance to avoid computer disaster.

Tip: System Restore

First, your computer's operating system probably has built into it a *system restore* function. If it has been turned on before there is a problem, you can put your computer's system back into the state it was in on a prior date (hopefully before the problem arose). Second, you can get rollback software that does more and allows you to rewind your computer's clock and go back in time to uninstall new software (such as a computer virus) and maybe even also restore files that have been deleted or modified. Some rollback programs back up your data files and some don't.

Product Tips: Rollback Software

Norton GoBack is a data protection product that continually monitors changes to your computer system and lets you undo changes to your computer (i.e., it lets you go back to a previous state when your computer was working properly) by (a) restoring files that have been deleted, modified or overwritten and (b) helping your computer recover from faulty software installations. Symantec, www.symantec.com

Retrospect is a top-rated program that does rollback restores and more—it also does individual file backups, incremental backups and full system backups as well as full system restores. Individual computer and network versions (for up to three computers) are available. It has built-in data encryption and password protection. EMC Corp., www.dantz.com

While rollback software or system restore should *not* be your only backup tools, it's nice to have them as other arrows in your computer quiver.

One Dozen Ways to Boost Your Backup Routine

Although it's better to back up more often than less often, the reality is that the correct backup routine depends on how often your files change and how your business or life would function if you didn't have a copy of all your files. Here are some suggestions:

1. Get your computer ready to do a backup.

Do computer maintenance by deleting unneeded folders and files (including the cache — see Chapter 2) and archiving old files that don't need to be on your computer.

2. Always test out a new backup set or device.

When you first get and install a backup device, test it out with some junk files before betting your life on it.

To check if a backup was successful, randomly restore a few files from the start, middle and end of your backup set.

3. Each day back up any data, folders or applications you have modified that day.

4. Do a full backup of your data every week.

Keep a backup log of when and what you back up. Check for reliability before you need it by trying to restore a few files from a backup a couple times each month.

5. **Do a full backup of your active program files at least every one to three months.**

   Over time you'll update or upgrade these programs. Also make backup copies of your customization files, Registry and application configuration files.

   ### Tip: Faster Backups

   If all of your program files are grouped together (e.g., in the Programs folder on your C drive), it's faster to back them up from that one location.

6. **Have at least two complete backup sets of programs and data.**

   Keep one set on-site and an additional backup off-site (at home, for example, if your office is not in your home or if it is, then maybe on the Web).

7. **Make hard copy printouts of important files and information.**

8. **Always back up newly installed software.**

   This is particularly important if you took any special steps during the installation.

   ### Tip: Have Hard Copy Backups

   Keep a hard copy record of the answers you gave to installation questions in case you need to reinstall the program.

9. **Make an emergency start-up DVD or CD.**

   You'll want this emergency backup disk to get you up and running again on your existing computer or another computer. Your antivirus software or your operating system (e.g., Windows) may have built-in help to walk you through the creation of emergency disk(s).

10. **Your backup routine should include complete or full backups as well as selective backups.**

    Complete or *full backups* are used to copy the entire contents of your computer's hard disk and are useful to restore all the data and programs from your computer's hard disk. *Selective backups* only back up certain files or folders you select or just files that have changed since the last major backup.

11. **Know when to choose incremental vs. differential backups.** An *incremental backup* is a type of selective backup that copies only files that have changed since your last (full or incremental) backup.

> ### Tip: Incremental Backups and a Backup Trail
> Incremental backups save each backed-up version of a file. You may want this approach if you ever need to refer to one of these versions or want to have an audit trail. Also see the warning below under Image Backups on trying to combine image backups, defragging *and* incremental backups.

A *differential backup* contains all the changes to a file since your last full backup and puts them in one file rather than having many incremental files. If you don't need to see old versions but only the most current, up-to-date version, use differential backups. Personally, on important work, we like to have many versions of a document in case a file gets corrupted, so we prefer incremental backups.

12. **Know when to choose image vs. file-by-file backups.**

Image backups make a mirror-image copy of your computer's hard disk. They copy your entire hard disk, byte by byte, so this everything-*including*-the-kitchen-sink approach isn't generally used for day-to-day backups due to the time it takes to make a complete disk backup. They are more often used for major, periodic backups.

This type of backup can be very useful when a hard disk crashes and you want backup files that contain an exact copy of your computer's hard disk, including all the computer data, operating system and program information.

> ### Image Backup and Defrag Warning
> If you make a full image backup and then defragment

your disk, you can't make just an incremental image backup. The reason is that all those bits and bytes have been moved around by the defragging and location matters when it comes to an image backup. The simple solution is to do another full image backup. That's a good idea anyway because if you suffer the trauma of a hard disk crash, it's easier and more straightforward to restore one complete image rather than an initial image and incremental additions.

File-by-file backups, while generally slower to make than image backups, are more reliable and make it easier to find backed-up files. You can also restore individual files without having to restore the entire hard disk. Newer technology is aiming for faster, file-by-file backups. File-by-file backups can be used for selective as well as complete backups.

Selecting a Backup Device, Medium or Location

Six Criteria

Before you select a device to back up your computer, consider the following criteria:

1. Capacity

Be sure to match or, better yet, exceed the capacity of your computer(s). Determine not only how much space you need now but also in the foreseeable future.

2. Internal vs. external

If an external device has enough capacity, it can back up more than one computer.

3. Ease of use and convenience

If it's not easy to learn and use, you won't bother with it. Can you do one-touch backups where you just push one button?

4. **Speed**

    How much of your time will it take to back up? How fast is it in different modes of operation—with or without compression, with or without *verification* (error checking)?

5. **Reliability/verification**

    Find out what kind of error checking it has so you know you can rely on it as a backup medium.

6. **Cost of the device**

    Costs have come way down on internal and external hard drives.

Types of Backup Devices and Places (Including Online Storage)

You have a wide choice of devices and places—internal hard drives, external hard drives, DVDs, CDs, Zip drives, tape, USB thumb drives, memory cards, mobile devices, iPods and online storage. They all have their pros and cons in terms of capacity, speed, cost, universality and durability. We'll examine the best ones at the present time.

> ### Tip: Disk Devices Have Many Advantages
> In general, disk devices are generally fast in terms of backup speed, economical in cost and offer a good life span.

Hard Disks

You'll probably want a second hard disk (external or internal) for backups. Prices have dropped tremendously on these drives and their storage capacity is ever increasing.

> ### Tip: External Hard Drives
> We're partial to external hard drives. Besides offering large capacity and the capability of being stored off-site, one drive can be used to back up several of your computers, including laptops. You may want to have two external drives so you can keep one off-site.

Some computers come with a slot for a removable hard disk. This can also be a good way to store sensitive information overnight by locking up the removable hard disk in a safe or taking it with you.

Partition Warning

Stay away from using another partition on the same hard drive as the backup location. The risk here is that if the drive fails, the files on both your main drive and the extra backup partition may be unusable. Get an external drive instead. They're so inexpensive they're a bargain you can't refuse.

Optical Media (CDs, DVDs, High Capacity DVDs and Holographic Drives)

Depending upon the type of optical media and the size of your file backup needs, optical media may work for you as a backup medium. With any kind of optical storage, check with the manufacturer to determine how long your data will remain usable.

CDs only hold about 700 MB—less than three-quarters of one gigabyte (1 GB). There are two types of CDs—rewritable (CD-RW) and one time recordable (CD-R). For laptop computers, a CD or DVD drive is often the only built-in backup device with DVD drives becoming more common.

Although DVD disks cost more than CD disks, a regular DVD can hold 4.7 GB (nearly seven times as much as a CD) and a dual-layer disk can hold around 8.5 GB. The newer, second generation high-capacity DVDs can hold 15 to 25 GB in a single-layer capacity and 30 to 50 GB in dual-layer capacity, depending upon the disk format. Holographic discs will initially store hundreds of gigabytes and capacity will increase over time.

Multiple Format Warning

Because there are two main formats for the first-generation DVDs, the plus (+) and minus (–) formats, there may be compatibility issues with DVDs. Get a DVD burner and drive that meets your needs and works with *all* your equipment. There are currently two competing formats (Blu-ray and HD-DVD) for second-generation DVDs.

USB Drives

We're most partial to the very small USB thumb drives. They're easy to use (just insert one into a USB slot on your computer and copy files or folders) and they provide up to multi-gigabyte capacity.

Some of these drives are now like having a computer in your pocket. In time it will be standard for all these drives to include software applications (some do now). Another advantage of this format (unlike CDs or DVDs) is that you don't need to burn in the information to copy it. The main downside is the possibility of losing these small devices. Some people wear them dangling on a cord around their neck to avoid losing them.

> ### Tip: USB Speeds
> Make sure both your computer and USB thumb drive have a fast USB connection (USB 2.0 is 40 times faster than the older USB 1.1).

Two possible downsides of a USB drive can occur when you plug this drive into someone else's computer. First, unless you take some steps in advance, using someone else's computer has the risk of leaving traces of your data on the host computer. Increasingly, USB drives and software are being specially designed to prevent this from happening. Second, your USB drive may pick up a virus.

> ### Product Tip: USB Device Protection Software
> *P.I. Protector Mobility Suite* software loaded on a USB flash drive is designed to give you protection. Imagine LAN, Inc., 800/372-9776 [NH] or www.imaginelan.com

> ### Product Tip: Protected USB Drives
> The *M-Trust Drive* is designed to securely store and encrypt sensitive information. M-Systems, Ltd., www.m-systems.com

See Chapter 2 for more ways to protect your USB drives.

Online Backup and Storage

Online storage can be a great off-site backup option but speed and cost can be issues depending on how much you have to back up.

The speed of your online connection will affect not only how long it takes to do a backup but also how likely you are to do regular backups.

If you have a fast enough Internet connection and the storage/backup charges meet your budget, a secure Web-based backup offers the benefit of being off-site but also accessible from any Internet connection.

As with anything online, check out the security measures in place. Also find out the backup capacity size, whether you can back up your entire computer's contents or just certain data files, whether files are compressed (try to avoid this, if possible, since uncompressing is just one more step that can go wrong), whether they're encrypted, how many versions of files are retained and how long they're retained online.

Finally, see the *Online Storage Warning* earlier in this chapter.

Product Tips: Online Backup Storage

If you're looking for online backup storage, see whether these companies can meet your budget and your needs for capacity, security and speed:

IBackup gives you flexible options. Pro Softnet Corp., www.ibackup.com

Streamload offers fee and free online storage space. Streamload, Inc., www.streamload.com

Tip: Email Account Storage

You may have enough online storage with your email account (e.g., Google's Gmail) for your most critical online storage needs by sending yourself emails with attached files.

Online Storage Warning

Don't rely solely on online backups. If you use online storage, you should also have backups in your physical possession (e.g., on an external hard drive) for another reason. Your online photos, other images and information may be destroyed by the online service or become inaccessible to you under the terms and conditions of the online vendor. And if an online provider goes bankrupt, you may lose access, too. Read the fine print before you sign up for online storage arrangements, especially free and/or unlimited storage arrangements. In some cases, for example, your photos may be deleted by the online storage vendor if you don't purchase a minimum amount of services or log in and view your images within a specified period of time (e.g., every 90 days). At the time this book is being written, in the case of Yahoo!, if you die, no one has access to your photos or emails stored online (see the *No Right of Survivorship and Non-Transferability* paragraph in the Yahoo! Terms of Service).

Backup Software

You can use the built-in backup software within your computer's operating system, or better yet, a third-party backup software program or the backup program that comes with your backup device. The right software depends on, in part, the type of backup you'll be making.

No matter what software you use, always have on hand a CD with the backup software just in case disaster strikes.

Email Warning

Most backup programs save all of your emails in one file rather than as individual messages. Sometimes that can present a problem in accessing those backed up emails individually. One solution is to have an email account where the server saves an online copy of every message.

Product Tips: Backup Software Programs

Acronis True Image is an imaging program that can also do incremental and differential backups. Acronis, Inc., www.acronis.com

Norton Ghost is an imaging backup program that allows users to create exact replicas of the entire contents of their hard drive. Each image, or *recovery point*, can be archived offline and used to restore the computer hard disk to exactly the way it was when the recovery point was taken. Symantec, www.symantec.com

Retrospect is a top-rated program that does rollback restores, individual file backups, incremental backups and full system backups as well as full system restores. Individual computer and network versions (for up to three computers) are available. It has built-in data encryption and password protection. EMC Corp., www.dantz.com

SyncBackSE is an award-winning backup and synchronization program that allows you to easily and automatically back up any file (pictures, videos, music, Word documents, spreadsheets, databases, emails) including open files you're working on. 2BrightSparks Pte Ltd., www.2brightsparks.com

Video File Backups

Due to their large sizes, video files may require a different backup solution. You may want to keep these files on a separate partition (portion of your hard drive) or on a separate hard drive. This will speed up the backup of your nonvideo data files since you won't have to back up both types each time you do a backup.

Tip: Use Uncompressed File-by-File Backups

To have faster and easier access, you'll usually make an uncompressed file-by-file backup rather than a compressed, image backup of video files.

Since video files gobble up hard disk space, you're more likely to be archiving this type of data. With archiving, you're removing noncurrent video files from your computer and putting them in storage.

Disaster Prevention and Recovery

Although good file and folder organization, computer housekeeping and good backups can help prevent disasters, here are a few other tips that can help.

1. **Wait a while after adding a software program or any hardware.**

   Make sure what you add is working well before adding anything else; otherwise, it can be difficult to unscramble problems.

2. **Make a backup before you install *any* new software.**

3. **During a power outage, don't just turn off your PC.**

   Unplug it and all the attached peripherals.

4. **Never reformat your drive without first testing your backup files.**

5. **Be careful about movement.**

   Don't move or bump a drive while it's in operation (and wait a minute for a hard drive to stop spinning before you move it). Carefully transport a removable drive in a padded case to prevent harmful movement.

If you need help restoring a file, a drive or an entire computer's contents that has been accidentally deleted, there are companies in the business of restoring data. There is also software that can do this to a more limited degree.

Product Tips: File and Disk Repair and Recovery Programs and Services

DriveSavers, in the business of data recovery since 1985, rescues data from crashed and broken hard drives and other storage media. DriveSavers Data Recovery, Inc., 800/440-1904 [CA] or www.drivesavers.com

EasyRecovery DataRecovery can recover lost, inaccessible or deleted data. OnTrack DataRecovery, www.ontrack.com

File Restore can undelete and restore files cleared from the Recycle Bin. Winternals Software, LP, www.winternals.com

Search and Recover is designed to recover files even after the Recycle Bin is emptied; recover data from formatted drives even after Windows is reinstalled; recover data after a virus attack, partitioning error or computer crash; recover data from hard and floppy drives, CD/DVD media, cameras, music players and memory cards; and on the other side of the coin, securely delete any file or folder, overwriting it up to 100 times. Iolo Technologies, LLC, www.iolo.com

SpinRite is a stand-alone program designed to refurbish hard drives and recover data from marginally or completely unreadable hard drives and from partitions and folders that have become unreadable. Gibson Research Corp., www.grc.com

Undelete replaces the Windows recycle bin and intercepts all deleted files, no matter how they were deleted. It can even restore your earlier, saved-over versions of Microsoft Office (Word, Excel, PowerPoint) files. It also includes *SecureDelete*, an electronic shredder to completely erase confidential files. Diskeeper Corp., www.undelete.com

Synchronization ("Syncing") with a Mobile Device

If you have a mobile device as well as a computer where you want the same data on both, you'll want to have another type of backup known as *synchronization* or *syncing* and you'll probably want to do it daily. With synchronization, all of your electronic devices have the same data (e.g., calendar, customer information, product information, etc.). There are different ways that software programs and websites provide synchronization.

Before buying a mobile device, it's important to determine how easy (or difficult) it will be to synchronize the device with all of your equipment. This is an area of great change with new approaches that make the process more automatic and effortless.

How It Works

Data may be updated on one device at a time, several at the same time or with each device receiving the latest information automatically each time it's turned on. You also may be able to drag and drop files between the devices without having to go through the entire data synchronization process and possibly utilize wireless (and cradle-less) synchronization through Wi-Fi and/or Bluetooth wireless technologies.

There will be times when you need to connect up remotely to your computer or to work with others. The next two chapters cover long-distance computing.

Part 5

When You Can't Dance Cheek-to-Cheek

Long Distance Computing

14

Remote Computing: Working with Yourself

When you first learned to dance, you probably spent some time practicing by yourself to improve your moves. For many of us, personal computers started out as solitary activities, too. Just you and the screen.

Now the drive to communicate electronically all the time with others through email, instant messages, text messages, VoIP, online conferencing, Web pages, blogs, intranets, wikis, RSS feeds and community search sites with tagging is satisfying that human need to be connected. Maybe that's why no matter what the dance craze is, slow dancing never goes out of style. We all want to be linked to other people. It's more fun that way.

Part 5 shows how we can be better linked to ourselves through remote control and remote access software (covered in this chapter) and with others via collaborative computing software (see chapter 15).

Remote Access and Remote Control Programs

It may not be enough to have a mobile device or a laptop computer with you while you're away from the office. What you may need is access to *all* the information that is on your main office computer (i.e., your desktop computer) or your company's computer network. Even if you've synchronized your desktop data with your mobile device before taking off, while you're away from the office that desktop data may keep changing. And you may also need access to all of the software programs on your main office computer.

Glossary
The computer with the files, information and software programs on it that you want to access is known as the *host* computer. The computer you're using to access the host computer is called the *client* computer. With both remote control and remote access software, the host computer must be turned on and connected to the Internet so the client computer can connect up to it.

Speed Warning
You need a fast enough Internet connection to make the experience at least tolerable, if not enjoyable.

Differences between Remote Access and Remote Control Software

There are two types of programs to connect to a host computer: remote access and remote control programs. Although both types of programs are sometimes labeled as remote access, there can be a

difference. Unless you need to use applications or networked resources on the host computer, remote access software may be all you
require.

With *remote access* software, you can access and forward your email,
files and PIM data from the host computer via the Internet using a
browser viewer. With Web-based remote access programs, special
software is not required on the client computer and you can access
your files, emails and PIM data. With some programs (e.g., *LapLink
Everywhere*), you can even remotely access this data using a Web-
enabled Smartphone or PDA.

With *remote control* software, you're actually taking long-distance
control of the host computer (including all the applications and files
on it) via the Internet or a network. Using a Web browser or remote
control software, it's like you're sitting at the desktop of the host
computer with total access to all your software programs, too.

With some remote control programs, you need to have the software
installed on both the host and client computers. That can present a
problem, for example, if you're borrowing a computer that doesn't
have the remote control software installed on it.

By contrast, with Web-based remote control programs, a small Java or
ActiveX program downloads automatically onto the client computer,
allowing you to use any computer to remotely control your host
computer.

Different remote control and remote access solutions can be variously
compatible with PCs, Macs and even mobile devices.

Product Tips: Remote Software
GoToMyPC is Web-based remote control software that
lets you see and access your actual main computer desktop and contents and work as if you were sitting right
there with access to all your file and network connections. Citrix Systems, Inc., www.gotomypc.com

LapLink Everywhere is both remote control and remote

access software that works with computers and mobile devices. You can access your remote PC even when it's protected by firewalls. LapLink Software, Inc., 800/527-5465 [WA] or www.laplink.com

LapLink Gold lets you connect to other LapLink-enabled computers over any connection type to access a PC's critical resources. You can remotely access files and folders; synchronize data between computers; run applications; support co-workers or friends; print files on distant printers; and operate, maintain and even reboot computers. You can access your remote PC even when it's protected by firewalls. LapLink Software, Inc., 800/527-5465 [WA] or www.laplink.com

MioNet lets you search, manage and access files or run backup programs on one computer or simultaneously across all your computers using a private network that is integrated with Windows. Senvid, Inc., www. senvid.com

MyWebExPC offers Web-based remote control of your main computer. Just install MyWebExPC on the host computer. No software is required on the client computer. Access is all done through the browser. WebEx Communications, Inc., https://pcnow.webex.com

Borrowed Computer Warning

If you use someone else's (or a hotel business center's) computer to access the data on your main computer, keep security concerns in mind since you may be leaving a trail of passwords and other information on the host computer. (See Chapter 2 for ways to protect your information.)

File and Email Synchronization

If your goals are more modest and you're just looking to share or synchronize files and/or emails between two computers, there are solutions available. Some are just for files while others handle both emails and files.

Product Tips: File Sharing/Synchronization

Avvenu gives you remote access to the files and photos on your computer from a mobile device or another computer. It automatically formats images to the device you're using. Avvenu, Inc., www.avvenu.com

BeinSync keeps your files *and* emails in sync between your PCs so they are always available and easily shared — all without resorting to sending yourself emails or using remote access products. If you're traveling without a laptop, BeinSync also supports remote Web access. BeinSync, Ltd., www.beinsync.com

EasyReach provides a remote desktop search service that enables you to instantly find any file or email on your work or home PCs using a BlackBerry, smartphone or Internet browser. EasyReach is designed to perform at its best on mobile devices. EasyReach Corp., www.easyreach.com

FolderShare automatically synchronizes file changes between linked computers. It allows you to create a private peer-to-peer network that will help you synchronize files across multiple devices and access or share files with business colleagues or friends. You no longer need to send large files via email, burn them to CDs/DVDs and mail them or upload them to a website. FolderShare allows you to share and sync important information instantly with anyone you invite. Byte Taxi, Inc., www.foldershare.com

Google Desktop lets you search files across multiple computers and also store and access the files online from Google servers. See Chapter 2 for a discussion of related security issues. Google, Inc., www.google.com

SyncToy for Windows XP is a free Microsoft download that lets you copy, move and synchronize folders between a computer and other devices such as a USB thumb drive. SyncToy is a more powerful version of Windows Briefcase that's built into Windows Explorer. Microsoft Corp., www.microsoft.com (search for *synctoy*)

Web-Based Multifunction Software

For some of us, our computing future will only be using and accessing software and data stored on the Web and not on our computers. The obstacles that need to be overcome are bandwidth, speed, accessibility and privacy concerns.

In the meantime, look for new, Web-based technology such as *Glide Effortless* (Transmedia Corp., www.glidedigital.com). Offering a compatible browser-based environment, Glide Effortless is designed to provide a portable desktop that links with your current desktop; online meetings through a virtual meeting and media-sharing forum; online storage space; uploading, managing, storing and sharing of online video, music, image and document files that are greatly reduced in size to overcome email file-attachment limitations; sharing contacts and calendars; and more.

There are exciting ways to work with others that can improve productivity and save you time. Collaborative computing is covered in the next chapter.

15

Collaborative Computing: Working with Others

It takes two to tango but two or more can collaborate at the same time over the Internet. Computer technology can improve how you collaborate—work, communicate, share information and build teamwork with others—in four main areas:

1. Online meetings and conferencing

2. Online file and document sharing

3. Online project management

4. Online sharing of ideas and thoughts

Online meetings let you collaborate, share and discuss projects, policies, sales approaches, documents, files or whatever in *real time*.

File sharing can include real-time collaboration, getting notifications of file changes by others, synchronizing file changes and online chatting with others about the files.

With online project management, you can coordinate the scheduling, planning and management of projects and have a central place for all team members to keep track of the individual steps as well as the overall progress.

With wikis and other idea sharing avenues, community bulletin boards can replace email in part and expand the breadth of online discussions. (A *wiki* is a website that allows many people to add and revise information; akin to a gigantic community or company bulletin board, it functions like an online whiteboard.)

Online (Virtual) Meetings —Web Conferencing

Web conferencing refers to holding group meetings over the Internet with each participant at a computer. Usually, participants see what's on the presenter's screen and use a telephone conference call, VoIP (using Internet telephone capability) or text chat to augment the video image. It is two-way communication and meant to simulate all persons being in the same room at the same time. One way to try out this approach is with VoIP calls that include video capability.

Using technology for distance meetings has become more common and more advanced. Especially with the expense of traveling, face-to-face meetings are being cut back because they are more often seen as a drain on productivity, time and the bottom line. As a result, virtual meeting software will become even more important in the coming years.

Remember that although virtual meetings remove geographic barriers, they don't eliminate different time zones. No one enjoys a 5 a.m. online meeting.

Tip: Use a Virtual Meeting When It's Right

Before scheduling a meeting, make sure a Web meeting is appropriate. A face-to-face meeting may be more appropriate especially for an initial contact with someone. Perhaps the biggest downside to online meetings is the loss of direct eye contact, which is so important in communication. Two-dimensional online conferencing tools are not the same as the three-dimensional feedback of being there when it comes to reading body language and facial expressions.

Bandwidth Warning

Bandwidth is very important. If some participants have dial-up rather than high-speed connections, the software may not work well. In some cases, firewalls present problems.

Security Warning

As with anything online, security is important. It may not be enough to have encryption for the images and files being transmitted. If you're using VoIP so the Internet provides your telephone connection, a secure connection is essential there, too.

Web Conferencing Features

Web conferencing can range from plain vanilla communication to all the bells and whistles. It can include some or all of the following:

- Video
- Audio
- Text chat
- VoIP
- Animation
- Polls
- Surveys

- Ways to create notes, action items and minutes including *whiteboarding* (an interactive, digital whiteboard where meeting notes can be instantly recorded, saved and shared in real time over the Internet)

- Meeting controls

- Passwords and security controls

- Waiting rooms for participants waiting for permission to join the group

- Ways to mute or eject participants

- Integration with your other software programs

- Wireless or wired connections

Web Conferencing Software and Services

There is software as well as services to help you put on real-time presentations and collaborate across the Internet.

Product Tips: Web Conferencing Software and Services

GoToMeeting is a Web-based online meeting service that has just about all you could want. Citrix Systems, Inc., www.gotomeeting.com

Microsoft Office Live Meeting is a hosted Web conferencing service that lets you hold virtual meetings with anyone, anytime, anywhere with just a phone, a computer and an Internet connection.
Microsoft Corp., www.microsoft.com

NetMeeting is an Internet conferencing solution for Windows users with features including remote computer control, multiple program sharing, multi-point data conferencing, text chat, whiteboard and file transfer as well as point-to-point audio and video. Microsoft Corp., www.microsoft.com/windows/netmeeting/

WebEx Meeting Center is a leading online conferencing service. It is flexible and powerful. WebEx Communications, www.webex.com

Product Tip: Digital Whiteboard

mimio Xi (a portable device that attaches to any whiteboard) and *mimioBoard* (a 4' x 6' whiteboard with digital whiteboarding technology built in) both let you capture and share whiteboard notes, collaborate in real time over the Internet and control projected presentations from the board, away from your computer. Virtual Ink Corporation, www.mimio.com

Online Sharing of Files, Documents and Information

Document sharing capabilities start with your word processing program and then get more sophisticated.

Tracking Changes

On its simplest level, your word processing program (and possibly other programs) probably has a tracking changes collaborative tool.

How to Use It

For example, in Microsoft Word, go to the *Tools* menu and select *Track Changes*. This feature will track additions and deletions you make to a document.

Then any changes you make are highlighted. After you save the changes (make sure you use the "Save As" command when you save the corrections to the file so you don't overwrite the original file), you can email the revised file.

The receiver, using Track Changes, can review, accept or reject your changes in Word and then make additional changes. Your word processing program may also have an option under the file menu to "send to" an email recipient or online meeting participant.

Simple tools have their limits. The track changes tool can become cumbersome when the number of collaborators increases. Even if everyone remembers to turn on the track changes feature before making edits, it can be difficult to work with a document that has been touched by too many hands. If that's the case, look for worksharing software to use with your word processor.

Product Tip: Worksharing Software Used With Word

Workshare lets you see changes to Word documents and who made the changes. Workshare, Inc., 415/293-9809 [CA] or www.workshare.com

Online Document Sharing

With this type of system, you share documents that are stored, retrieved, distributed, managed and archived over the Internet. The documents might be available to every employee in your company or permissions might be set up for individual files or certain storage areas. Systems vary in the file types supported; whether there's version control so you can keep track of who changed what; and the level of security.

PDF and XML File Formats

There are more universal file formats that can preserve the formatting and let you read (and possibly edit) the document without having the original software that created the document or other special software. The main universal formats are *PDF* (portable document format) and *XML* (extensible markup language). These formats can provide a way to share and reuse information and data across applications, platforms and the Internet.

Product Tip: Online Collaboration Tool

Writeboard lets you create and store shareable Web-based text documents, save every version, roll back to earlier versions, compare changes and work with yourself on the documents or collaborate with colleagues. 37signals LLC, www.writeboard.com

The Evolution of Collaborative Computing

What seemed productive yesterday for collaboration (sending files as attachments to emails) pales with the next stage of working with someone else.

Whether you're communicating across the world or to an office down the hall, you want everyone to be on the same page...literally, and at the same time. That means using software that shows the same document on both screens so you can see onscreen editing and changes by each other in real time (as compared to emailing versions as attached files).

Today two or more people using the Internet can work simultaneously with the same document or graphic on each screen and interact with one another. *Groove* (see below) is an example of a program that allows this real-time interaction. (Another method that may become more popular as a collaborative approach is using private RSS feeds [see Chapter 9] to keep team members advised of developments and document revisions.)

Groupware software allows teams and colleagues to work together on projects even when they are separated geographically.

Product Tips: Groupware

Colligo enables any laptop or Pocket PC to instantly network to one or more computers using a 802.11 wireless connection. You can create an instant network with one click. Once connected, you can share files, send messages, share an Internet connection, share a printer, compare calendars, replicate databases and more. Colligo offers a personal edition, a workgroup edition and a workgroup edition with a Lotus Notes plug-in. Colligo Networks, Inc., www.colligo.com

Groove allows groups of workers to share information and files; collaborate over intranets and the Internet; have

conversations; post questions and get answers about files and projects; receive notifications when files change; and hold meetings. Groove lets participants see changes to open documents as they happen. Groove will be renamed as Office Groove 2007 in the next version of Office, Microsoft Office 2007.
Microsoft Corp., www.microsoft.com

HotOffice stores files in one central online location for remote access, revision control and keyword search. In addition, the software lets you share ideas on private company bulletin boards. Emails and calendars can be consolidated or kept private and private or group reminders and meetings can be scheduled. Thruport Technologies, Inc., 703/914-9700 [VA] or www.hotoffice.com

IBM Lotus Notes pioneered the groupware category. Notes is not an application but rather the leading groupware application platform used for building and delivering a wide range of applications. Programmers and other highly technical people use IBM Lotus Notes directly to build custom, corporate or groupware applications. Notes helps keep critical information (in a variety of different formats) moving to everyone in an organization who needs it. IBM, www. lotus.com/notes

IBM Lotus QuickPlace (formerly known as *IBM Lotus Team Workplace*) is designed to let users instantly create secure teamrooms and work spaces on the Web, providing them with a "place" to coordinate people, tasks, plans and resources; collaborate; and communicate on any project or ad hoc initiative. IBM, www.lotus.com/quickplace

IBM Lotus Sametime (formerly called *IBM Lotus Instant Messaging and Web Conferencing*) allows real-time collaboration over the Internet. You can see, in advance, whether a person is available to collaborate; use instant messaging to converse in real time through text, audio and/or video; and conduct Web conferences to share presentations, applications or the entire desktop. IBM, 800/343-5414 [MA] or www.lotus.com/sametime

IBM Workplace Collaboration Services is a single product combining various collaboration tools that support the different ways people interact with each other during a typical work day — online, real-time or in person. Workplace Collaboration Services provides the flexibility to deploy any mix of capabilities at any time, anywhere, depending upon the user's needs. Collaboration capabilities include email; calendaring; instant messaging; Web conferencing; team spaces; learning; Web content management; shared document libraries; productivity editors (spreadsheets, presentations etc.); and templates. In addition, it features a new activity and process centric collaboration tool called *Activity Explorer* that enables users to associate related exchanges together as activities. IBM, www.ibm.com/software/workplace/collaborationservices

WebEx Meeting Center lets you share applications, presentations, documents — even your desktop — in real time within a Web browser so you can hold online meetings from any computer with a network connection. You can collaborate with remote coworkers and annotate or edit documents in real time. With a telephone and an Internet connection, you can hold a WebEx meeting. No additional hardware or software is required since WebEx Meeting Center is a Web-based hosted service. WebEx Communications, www.webex.com

Windows Shared View and *Windows Meeting Space*, programs in Windows Vista, are designed to allow for document collaboration. These programs are in beta testing as this book is being written. Microsoft Corp., www.microsoft.com

Online Project Management

Some companies handle project management through online shared calendars, schedules, task tracking and resource allocation. Others use online discussion groups and forums along with document sharing to move projects along. Still others use dedicated project management applications.

Product Tips: Project Management Software

Basecamp is a more fully-featured Web-based project management tool. *Backpack* is Basecamp's little brother that's better suited to personal or smaller projects such as gathering in your ideas, notes and files online. 37signals, LLC, www.basecamphq.com and www.backpackit.com

Microsoft Project 2003 is a family of products, including a Web-based component, to help you manage work and people. Microsoft Corp., www.microsoft.com

Online Sharing of Ideas and Thoughts

Other online collaborative tools to exchange ideas include wikis, blogs, intranets, extranets and instant messaging.

Security Warning

Just be sure whatever online technology you choose offers a secure connection and any needed encryption.

Wikis

Growing in number and importance in the work environment, wikis are a flexible tool that can be used as a company repository of useful information about products, customers and trouble-shooting solutions. Unlike a traditional website that requires a webmaster to input changes, with a wiki employees can click on the edit button to add their input directly.

Wikis are collaborative efforts so it's important to have ways for the posted information to be reviewed by peers and edited regularly to keep the information accessible and on point. And, of course, there is now *wam* (wiki spam).

Product Tips: Wikis

JotSpot is an application wiki that makes it easier to create and share Web pages, work together and keep in sync. You can create an intranet, manage projects, collaborate on documents, share calendars, create a help desk or knowledgebase and more. JotSpot, Inc., www.jot.com

JotSpot Tracker is a spreadsheet wiki. You can share spreadsheets online without creating multiple versions and handle tasks such as managing projects. JotSpot, Inc., http://tracker.jot.com

PMWiki is simple to install, customize and maintain. PmWiki, www.pmwiki.org

SocialText Workspace software can set up an enterprise wiki. SocialText, Inc., www.socialtext.com

Blogs and Vlogs

Weblogs (more commonly known as a *blogs*) started out as individual diaries on personal Web pages. You never know who may be reading your blog, maybe even your employer. There's even a term, *dooced*, for getting fired for blog entries. On a more positive note, now some companies are hiring professional bloggers to write copy on company sites that presents information and news in a more personal, interesting and informal way. Some blogs are interactive and allow comments while others are noninteractive. The format of blogs varies and usually includes links to other useful information. Video blogs (known as *vlogs*) are exploding in popularity. Finally, be on guard for spam blogs which are known as *splogs*.

Product Tip: Blog Publishing Software

WordPress software helps you design and publish your blog. This personal publishing platform gets your blogging from your computer on to the Web. WordPress, http://wordpress.org

Intranets

An intranet is an internal, corporate computer network that uses Internet features such as email, Web pages and browsers to build a private communications and data resource center for a specific company or organization. Built within its own firewall, an intranet is only accessible to the employees of that organization. Good intranets include specialized sites for different types of workers; for example, marketing and sales people would have some of their own sites, administrative people could have their own, etc. An effective, user-friendly intranet will also have simple keyword search functions. It should facilitate information sharing but not add to information overload.

Even though most large corporations are not using blogs, many of them are using blog technology instead of traditional intranets to turn their static websites into dynamic, interactive sites.

Extranets

An extranet is an intranet that's connected directly to a company's top customers and suppliers. Because it allows information to flow more freely between companies, efficiency and communication can be improved.

Instant Messaging

Your instant messenger program may offer audio and video conferencing. The usefulness of such conferencing depends on the quality of the audio and video output, the ability of video feeds to expand to full screens and the functionality to work with network firewalls. Over time, improvements will be made to the business conferencing capabilities of IM.

No matter where, how and with whom you work, you need to correctly select and use the right equipment. And with the way computer and mobile device technology keeps evolving, you won't want to miss the vital consumer guidelines and ergonomic information in Part 6 — The Box Step.

Part 6

The Box Step

Finding and Using
the Right Equipment

16

Ergonomics

The marathon dancing of the 1920s stretched people's endurance. Those endless, nonstop grueling competitions had people pushing themselves to get fame and fortune while exposing themselves to exhaustion, mental stress and physical problems. Sounds like a typical work day to us.

But if you want to avoid aches and pains and serious injuries from the modern-day marathon use of technology, learn how to position and use your computer, monitor, keyboard, mouse, telephone, desk and other furniture in ergonomically sound ways. Read this chapter to put yourself in the right position to get the most done with the least amount of strain and to recognize when enough's enough.

Ergonomics is the science of making the work environment compatible with people so they can work more comfortably and productively. Ergonomics looks at the dimensions, placement and use of equipment and matches them to the wide range of body sizes and shapes according to certain recommended standards.

213

Because you can do almost everything today at a computer, you may find that you are sitting there for more hours every day than ever before. But any single type of repetitive activity can be dangerous physically and mentally and lead to *repetitive stress/strain injury* (RSI).

Your goal with an ergonomic environment should be to avoid such symptoms as fatigue, eyestrain, blurred vision, headaches, stiff muscles, wrist pain, sore back, irritability and loss of feeling in fingers and wrists.

The longer you work at a desk or computer, the more you need to consider the importance of correct angles of eyes, arms, hands, legs and feet. Beyond avoiding health problems, there can be positive benefits, too. Some research indicates that the proper chair can add up to 40 productive minutes each work day and that means maybe you can cut down the length of your workday with the right equipment.

Tip: Avoid Lengthy Repetitive Activities
Avoid long periods of any repetitive activity whether it's keyboard use or making phone calls.

Start With Good Ergonomic Habits

Before looking at the nuts and bolts of setting up an ergonomic work space, we urge you to start by adopting more ergonomic work habits — take care of your body's health as you use computer technology each day.

Mobile Devices and Thumbs
Ergonomic standards and concerns can change over time as new studies are completed and new technology is introduced. One newer concern is how mobile devices such as smartphones and PDAs are changing how we use our fingers.

Thumbs are taking over some of the old jobs of index fingers. Overuse of thumbs can lead to repetitive stress/strain injury, especially if you do a lot of emailing or text messaging with your mobile device.

To help prevent this injury, the British Chiropractic Association designed a campaign called "How to Practice Safe Text" which recommended a series of simple "textercises" from a simple shoulder shrug to a finger spread and neck muscle stretch and included a list of texting tips.

Tip: Look for Voice Recognition Capability

Look for a mobile device with good voice recognition capabilities to handle common tasks so you don't end up all thumbs. And be on the lookout for the next big innovation—voice-text messaging where you can send text messages using your voice, not your thumbs.

MP3 Players and Ears

Another newer concern is hearing damage from listening to music on portable MP3 players. Although definite standards to avoid hearing problems have not yet been determined, preliminary research indicates that listening to loud music for even a very short period of time or even at a reduced volume setting for more than one-half hour per day is asking for trouble. Having the right headphones (as compared to the ear buds that are most often used) can help prevent problems. Be on the lookout for studies and recommendations on volume, time limits and strategies (e.g., certain headphones) to avoid problems.

The Eyes Have It

Your eyes need to roam during the day. Try these three ergonomic ideas for your eyes:

1. Pause every 20 minutes or so to look away from your computer or mobile device screen.

2. To prevent eyestrain, change your up-close focus by looking at distant objects.

3. Try to blink more often because blinking moistens your eyes and reduces eyestrain and we blink one-third as often while looking at text on a screen.

Product Tip: Computer Prescription Glasses

PRIO prescription eyeglasses are specifically designed

to reduce or eliminate computer-related vision problems including eyestrain, blurred/double vision and fatigue while viewing a computer screen. PRIO Corp., 800/621-1098 or www.prio.com

Stretching and Exercise Breaks

Don't be glued to your chair and desk. Take a short one to two-minute stretch break every 20 to 30 minutes. Every hour, take a "micro break" from typing for at least five minutes and stretch, stand up, walk around, make a phone call, think or just relax.

Product Tips: Computer Exercise and Reminder Software

Computer programs can be preset to pop up and remind you when it's time for a break or can even guide you through a variety of exercises.

Break Reminder, Chequers Software, Ltd, www.cheqsoft.com

RSI Guard, Remedy Interactive, 831/421-0139 [CA] or www.rsiguard.com

Set Up an Ergonomic Workspace

Work Surfaces

If you use one flat work surface for both writing *and* typing, be aware that most people prefer a writing surface that's higher than their ideal typing surface height.

Generally, people prefer a writing work surface 29 inches from the floor but a keyboard on a surface that's just 26 inches above the floor. If you just use a flat worksurface at the same height for both functions, you can't be at the best height at the same time for writing, keyboarding and mousing. Split-surface work designs, adjustable designs and keyboard/mouse tray systems can be especially helpful.

Chairs

Use a good ergonomic chair whose back and seat are adjustable. A good chair is more than a piece of furniture; it's a necessity for long hours of computer work. A bad one is literally a pain in the back.

It is generally recommended that the back of the chair be at a reclined angle of 110 degrees and that you have support for both your upper and lower back. The correct degree of reclining varies from person to person.

Experts differ on whether armrests help or create problems. If your chair has armrests, they should be adjustable, allow your shoulders to be relaxed and support your arms in a natural position.

Tip: Test Sit Chairs Before You Buy
Never buy a chair from a catalog; you should "test sit" any chair before you buy.

Telephones

Placement of your hard-wired desk telephone is an ergonomic factor that relates to left- or right-handedness and how long you typically use the phone each day.

Tip: Proper Placement of Desk Telephones
Should your telephone go on the right or left side of the desk if you are right-handed? In general, the correct answer is "left." Place your phone on the left so your right hand is free to write.

But if you're on the phone for long stretches of time, you should be using a telephone headset, in which case, placement may not be as critical. Get a telephone headset if you're on the phone at least two hours every day, you tend to have lengthy calls and/or you need your hands free for writing or typing while on the phone. A telephone headset can help prevent neck and back aches and trips to the chiropractor.

Tip: Getting the Right Headset
When it comes to headsets, compatibility with your

phone is critical. Either bring your phone to the store to test it or if you order a headset sight unseen, ask about compatibility and make sure the headset is completely refundable without any restocking or shipping/handling fee.

Product Tip: Headsets
Hello Direct has over 1,400 products on its site. Hello Direct, 800/435-5634 [CA] or www.hellodirect.com

Creating Privacy for Phone Calls
As an aside, we want to make you aware of a very useful telephone-related product. With today's cubicles, it can be difficult to have private conversations.

Product Tip: Voice Privacy Without Walls
Babble is designed to make the content of phone conversations unintelligible to passersby. Babble changes how other people hear your voice. It is designed to make your voice sound like a small crowd in a restaurant where no one outside your workspace can pick out specific words or understand your actual spoken words. Sonare Technologies (www.sonaretechnologies.com), a Herman Miller Company (www.hermanmiller.com)

Computers
Besides having your computer at the right height, it needs to be in the right position for you. If your computer is not on a desk right in front of you, do you prefer a computer on a left or right hand desk return (a small, narrow extension of a desk that is designed to hold a computer)?

Even a work surface has areas that are more convenient than others. Angle your computer, for example, off to the side for occasional use; place it right in front of you for frequent or constant use.

Special Considerations with Laptop Computers
Properly positioning a laptop computer can get tricky because the

screen, keyboard and mouse (touchpad) are all in one unit. With this fixed design, a good ergonomic position for the screen very often means that the keyboard or touchpad is not optimally placed and vice versa. So what can you do, especially if you use your laptop quite a bit?

Make sure you can see the screen without twisting your neck angle. (For more information on screen angle, see the next section on "Computer Displays—Monitors and Screens.") Once the screen is in a good position, then consider using separate, *external* devices for the keyboard and mouse to give yourself better ergonomic positioning especially if you're using your laptop as a desktop substitute. A laptop's all-in-one design doesn't produce a comfortable fit for most people, who end up hunching over their computers in unnatural positions. Such positions can strain your body as well as your eyes.

Also, make sure your laptop isn't heating up too much for its own good or your lap's.

> **Tip: Laptop Cooling Pads**
> Get a cooling pad with a fan that helps reduce your laptop's temperature.

If you carry your laptop along with other devices and accessories (e.g., an extra battery), it can become a luggable, not a portable computer, which can be very hard on your body. Use a computer bag on wheels to lighten your load.

Computer Displays—Monitors and Screens
Proper Placement
In general, you want your computer display to be as far away as possible where you can still read screen text clearly. For most people, that means placing the monitor or screen at least an arm's length away. Get a display that can tilt so you can adjust it to the proper angle for your eyes.

The first goal with monitors and screens is keeping your neck relaxed by not putting pressure or strain on it. That means you'll want the center of your monitor or screen right in front of you so you're looking at it straight on without turning your back or neck. Generally, your head and eyes should be positioned so you're not straining to hold your head up or down while you're typing and the display is at, or more likely, below eye level. Adjust the display angle and height to get the right fit for you.

Product Tip: Computer Display Adjuster

Pivot Pro software lets you rotate your computer's display between landscape and portrait orientations making it easier to adjust documents, email and Web browsing pages to the best viewing angle. Portrait Displays, Inc., 925/227-2700 [CA] or www.portrait.com

If you wear bifocals or blended glasses while using your computer, you may want to lower the monitor or screen even more to your reading level to avoid having to lift your head to do your typing. A better solution may be to get dedicated computer glasses that are optimized for use with a computer display, as discussed earlier in this chapter.

Preventing Eyestrain

The second goal with monitors and screens is to avoid eyestrain. You can reduce glare by using an LCD monitor or screen and correctly positioning the computer display to minimize glare from sources of light.

Glare can be direct or reflected. Reduce the glare from windows, overhead lights and task lights by putting the computer display at right angles to windows, adjusting the blinds or curtains, changing the screen angle and controls and using antiglare filters (if your computer display doesn't already have one). Depending on how they're angled and directed, task lights can increase or decrease glare.

You may also need to adjust the contrast and brightness of your monitor or screen. Eyestrain can also come from too much contrast. Laptops that feature very bright screens with a high contrast may produce too much glare for you.

Product Tip: Monitor Calibration Software

DisplayMate is top-rated monitor diagnostic and calibration software that lets you adjust, set up, calibrate, tune up, test, evaluate and improve image and picture quality. DisplayMate Technologies Corp., 800/932-6323 or www.displaymate.com

Higher Screen Resolutions and Smaller Font Sizes

LCD monitors and screens are getting larger in size and having higher resolutions. A higher resolution allows you to be productive by being able to put up more windows on the display. The bad news is that as LCDs get larger in screen size (e.g., above 17 inches) with the same high resolution, text on the display may shrink in size. If the text is too small, this could lead to eyestrain and also less productivity.

Tip: Ways to Increase Font Size

One easy approach to increase font size with your word processing program, for example, is to use the zoom feature—look for a percentage such as 100% at the top of the screen and adjust it upward to a higher percentage. (The next versions of Word and other Office applications are expected to have a sliding bar to adjust the size of text.)

Another approach that works with some programs and some websites is holding down the Ctrl (Control) key and rolling the scrolling wheel on your mouse to adjust the text size.

Other solutions include:

1. Changing the screen resolution to a lower setting (e.g., going from 1280 x 768 to 1024 x 768) via the control panel

2. Changing the font setting to a larger font size

3. Using the built-in "font smoothing" feature in the computer's operating system (for Windows XP, the

steps are: (1) Go to the desktop and right click in an open space, (2) click *Properties*, (3) click *Appearance*, (4) click *Effects*, (5) check the box that says *Use the following method to smooth edges of screen fonts,* (6) select *ClearType* in the dropdown list, (7) click *OK*, (8) click *Apply* and (9) click *OK*.

4. Using software programs to produce larger fonts

Product Tips: Font and Icon Enlarging Software

Liquid View increases the legibility of the Microsoft Windows interface so you can adjust the size of desktop icons, fonts, desktop toolbar and Microsoft application toolbars with the touch of a button, regardless of your display's native resolution. *Liquid Surf* lets you customize the appearance of Web content. You can increase or decrease the size of text and graphics within Internet Explorer. Portrait Displays, Inc., 925/227-2700 [CA] or www.portrait.com

Web Eyes can instantly change the text size and font of any website you visit. ION Systems, Inc., 800/983-6397 or www.webeyes.us

Advantages of LCD Monitors/Screens

Laptop computers come with LCD screens and now smaller footprint LCD monitors are more popular than traditional, free-standing large CRT monitors for desktop monitors, too.

LCD monitors/screens offer two ergonomic advantages. First, LCDs are easier on the eyes because they generally have less glare, are flicker free, give greater flexibility to adjust to your posture and improve visual work performance by reducing visual search and reading times. Second, LCDs do not emit electromagnetic radiation.

Keyboards

Your keyboard is one of the most important factors that determines just how happy you are with your computer as a whole.

Ergonomics come into play because RSI (repetitive stress/strain injury) is a concern with computer keyboards.

Tip: Get the Right Keyboard for You

Remember that no one keyboard or keyboard accessory is the right fit for everyone. Listen to your body when you're using a keyboard as to whether it's right for you. Your body type and size affects what feels comfortable to you. That's why "ergonomic" keyboards may be no better and may be worse for you than regular keyboards. If you're using a laptop computer, see whether an external keyboard puts less pressure on your hands and wrists.

Positioning Your Keyboard and Your Wrists

Just as you need to line up your monitor correctly, the same holds true for your external keyboard.

Position the most frequently used part of the keyboard with your monitor (for example, if you rarely use the numeric keypad portion off on the right side, you may want to center the rest of your keyboard so the "H" key lines up with the center of your body).

The keyboard height should allow your shoulders to be relaxed. An adjustable keyboard tray can help here. The tilt of your keyboard depends on how you're sitting.

When you're typing, your wrists ideally should be straight and level and not rest on anything. Avoid awkward angles. Avoid pounding the keys since that causes wear and tear on you.

Adapt a desk return that's too shallow with a keyboard extender or a keyboard drawer that mounts under a desktop and conveniently pulls out. A keyboard drawer is a space saver and depending on the type, can be a good accessory to lower a keyboard that's too high for comfortable typing. Articulating keyboard arms are similar to underdesk keyboard drawers but they usually have more adjustable positions, which may be a good idea if different people are using the same computer.

Product Tip: Keyboard Accessory
The *In-line Copyholder Underdesk Keyboard Drawer* maximizes valuable desk space and has a mouse platform. Kensington, 800/535-4242 [CA] or www.kensington.com

Wrist rests
Be careful if you select a wrist rest because it may not help you and may actually cause extra pressure on your wrists.

Reducing Keyboard Stress
Here are five ways to reduce keyboard stress:

1. **Take a five-minute break every hour to relax your hands.**

2. **Use macros.**
   A macro allows you to use as few as two keystrokes to replace many keystrokes or mouse clicks and is part of many computer programs.

3. **Use programmable keys that can remap the keys on your keyboard or define macros.**

4. **Use an external keyboard.**
   If you're using a laptop computer, see whether an external keyboard puts less pressure on your hands and wrists.

5. **Use voice recognition software to dictate text and give computer commands.**
   Just be sure you don't overuse your voice and strain it (or have inadvertent comments typed into your text).

   ### Tip: Write Using Voice Recognition
   Consider combining voice recognition software (for a first draft) with your keyboard and mouse (for edits).

   ### Product Tip: Voice Recognition Software
   Dragon NaturallySpeaking has been the best voice recognition product for years. Nuance Communications, Inc., www.nuance.com

Mouse Devices

Get a mouse whose design fits your hand. Look for (a) shapes and configurations that fit the size of your hands and fingers and (b) any features that reduce the amount of work your fingers, hands and arms need to do.

Try to get a mouse that is as flat as possible to reduce wrist extension. Avoid curved mice and see whether a larger mouse helps you make arm movements rather than wrist movements. Some people prefer a trackball mouse so a finger or thumb can control movements rather than a wrist. Ergonomic mice may help your wrist/hand posture. If you're left-handed, make sure you find a mouse that works for you. You may want a kid-sized mouse for your children to use.

Remember that it doesn't matter how ergonomically designed a product is; the final selection boils down to personal preference because one size or style does not fit all. Another new option is a mouse in the shape of a pen.

No matter which mouse you choose, don't squeeze or hold your mouse too firmly.

Reduce the Number of Mouse Clicks

One hundred clicks a day come to 36,500 clicks per year and nearly 200,000 over five years. Reducing the number of mouse clicks can save a lot of wear and tear on your body. Here's an easy way to eliminate maybe 100 mouse-clicks per day:

How to Reduce Mouse Clicks

Your computer's operating system may let you substitute single-clicking for double clicking. Here's how to do it in Windows XP (sorry, you have to do some mouse clicks now to reduce mouse clicks later):

1. Left click *My Computer*.

2. Left click *Tools*.

3. Left click *Folder Options*.

4. Click once in the bubble for *Single click to open an item*.

5. Left click *Apply*.

6. Left click *OK*.

Tip: Keyboard Shortcuts

Try also reducing the number of clicks by using *keyboard shortcuts* for various functions (e.g., to copy, center, bold, italicize, delete or save text) instead of using your mouse for these tasks. We think many computer injuries result from reaching for a mouse and using it too much. That's why we like using keyboard commands and shortcuts instead.

For a list of keyboard shortcuts for the 2003 versions of Microsoft Access, Excel, FrontPage, InfoPath, OneNote, Outlook, PowerPoint, Publisher, Visio and Word, go to *www.microsoft.com* and search for *HA011407361033.aspx*.

For Microsoft Word 2002 keyboard shortcuts, go to *www.microsoft.com* and search for *290938*.

Position Your Mouse Correctly

Place your mouse close to your keyboard so you don't have to reach upward or too far to use it. Ideally, have it on an angled platform just to the side of your keyboard or use a keyboard/mouse tray.

Look, too, for accessories that will position your mouse as close to the keyboard as possible so that if you're using a keyboard drawer or arm, you're not reaching for your mouse on the desktop. With keyboard trays that don't have enough room for a mouse, make sure you don't have to reach too far to get to your mouse. An external mouse may be physically less stressful than using a built-in touch pad.

Now that you know about positioning and using equipment ergonomically to help avoid injuries, you'll want to read Chapters 17 and 18 to find the best electronic tools to meet your needs.

17

Computers

We're not dancing solo these days. Machines and their technology are becoming our social partners. Cellphones, BlackBerrys and other mobile devices are almost extra limbs on our bodies the way they're attached to our belts, waists, hands and ears as our lifelines for constant communication with others. In fact, an article in MIT Technology Review by Wade Roush dubbed computers and mobile devices "social machines."

Computers have also become our second brains, storing and retrieving essential information and helping us analyze, think, write and explain.

We depend on computers wherever we are and want them accessible to us all the time. This will really be true in New Songdo City, which is being built in South Korea and will be the first *ubiquitous city* — an all-digital, networked city where all major information systems (residential, business, government and medical) will share data; computers will be built into houses, office buildings and streets; and the digital life will infuse everyday life with videoconferencing calls to neighbors and wireless access everywhere within the city.

Wherever and however you use computer technology, you need to partner up with the best equipment that meets your needs.

Laptops vs. Desktops

Laptop (notebook) computers now outsell desktops in the U.S. because a properly equipped laptop computer can do almost anything that a desktop computer can and it also offers mobility.

Over the years, we've become converts to laptop computers used as a desktop substitute. Our latest computers are nearly as powerful as any desktop and we can take them with us anywhere.

But because desktops have the space to hold multiple and larger hard drives, a desktop can be a speed demon when it comes to manipulating complex graphics and video, handling complicated number-crunching or playing high-end games.

Buying a laptop or a desktop computer generally involves the same factors with two major exceptions: (1) cost (a smaller laptop computer costs more for the same amount of computing power) and (2) portability (this factor only applies to laptops). The key subjective and objectives factors in buying a computer are covered below and at the end of the chapter in the Computer Buying Checklist.

The new ultra-compact, *ultra-mobile PCs* will be another option.

The Subjective Factors in Buying Any Computer—See, Touch and Feel

With a laptop or a desktop, you'll want a computer display (monitor or screen), mouse (or pointing device) and keyboard that works for you.

Monitors/Screens

Monitors and screens are like dance partners. You've got to see them in action and give them a spin to see whether they'll be a good match for you. A monitor/screen decision is important. One area where we've never compromised in over 20 years of computer ownership is screen clarity since we're in front of a computer for much if not most of each day. You may spend more waking time with your computer display than you do with your spouse or significant other.

Tip: Do a Test Run

Try out screens and monitors in a store one after another using the same tests. On each machine, type in the same words (in the same font and size) on the built-in word processing program (e.g., WordPad). Then call up the same photographs in the built-in graphics program (e.g., Paint). This will give you a sense of relative text and picture clarity of each display.

Tip: Do More Than Run the Numbers

With computer displays, you can't just look at the specification numbers. You have to look at the screens themselves. For example, text won't necessarily be as clear on two different displays with the same resolution specifications (e.g., 1280 x 768).

Tip: Higher Resolutions May Be Hard on Your Eyes

Keep in mind that as computer display resolutions get higher and sharper (larger numbers in the specifications — 1280 x 768 is a higher resolution than 1024 x 768), the fonts and other objects on the screen get smaller, maybe too small, unless you lower the resolution or use a software program to increase the font size (see Chapter 16). If you're looking at an LCD screen, find a screen resolution you like in its *native resolution*.

Tip: Check Out the Angles

Check out the viewing angles. Especially if you're using your computer display to make presentations to clients or customers, make sure they'll be able to see what you're showing.

Second Monitors and Multidisplay Software

If you're really in the mood to multitask, your operating system software (e.g., Windows) probably lets you run two displays off of one computer. (You may need to add a graphics card to do this.) You could run multiple applications to increase productivity such as with email on one monitor and your word processing program or Internet browser on the other one.

Product Tips: Multidisplay Software and Hardware

nView lets you specify which applications appear on each display. nVidia, www.nvidia.com

Dual Head 2 Go is a palm-sized, external multidisplay upgrade box that allows laptop users to upgrade to a multidisplay arrangement. Matrox Graphics, Inc., www.matrox.com/graphics

For more information on monitors and screens (dealing with ergonomics), see Chapter 16.

Mouse Devices

If you're not going to use an external mouse with a laptop, be sure the built-in pointing device feels good to you. Also, be on the lookout for mouse devices that offer a special feature such as the following one:

Product Tip: Magnifying Mouse

Microsoft's Wireless Optical Mouse 5000 can magnify the portion of the screen by the cursor and keep the rest of the screen at its unmagnified resolution. You can adjust the size and shape of the magnified area. Microsoft Corp., www.microsoft.com

For more information on computer mice (and ergonomics), see Chapter 16.

Keyboards

Keyboard feel (are the keys mushy or do they have the right amount of give?) is important for both desktop and laptop computers.

Tip: Laptop Keyboards Are Different

There are a couple of special factors with laptop keyboards. First, not all laptop keyboards have full-size keys. If you're a touch typist, it can throw you off to use smaller keys. Second, keys on a laptop built-in keyboard may be located in different places than on your external desktop keyboard. For example, the delete key on a built-in laptop keyboard may be more inaccessible because it is mixed in with other keys somewhere at the top of the keyboard. On an external keyboard, the delete key may be more prominent and closer to your fingers at the bottom of the keyboard.

Placement of keys on a laptop may not be as critical if you're going to use an external keyboard most of the time. Besides key placement, an external keyboard gives you the flexibility of placing the keyboard in a more comfortable position.

Soon it will be common to see LCD-based keyboards where each key will have a miniature LCD screen that can be programmed to display images, letters in different languages or perform computer functions.

For more on keyboards and ergonomics, see Chapter 16.

The Objective Factors in Buying a Computer—Specifications and Cost

How much computer you need depends upon what you're doing with the computer. Word processing, email and searching the Web are not very intensive functions so they don't require a very powerful chip to handle these tasks. However, number crunching and especially handling graphics and high-end games can call for more powerful (and maybe multiple) chips. The need for a large hard drive size shoots up dramatically if you're storing video and large graphic files as compared to small word processing files.

Tip: Speed and Security
Even if you don't need a fast computer for your work, a faster chip and hard drive can be very helpful in scanning for viruses and spyware more quickly. That means you're more likely to handle these essential tasks on a regular basis since they won't take as long to complete.

Use the Computer Buying Checklist at the end of this chapter to guide you when making your next computer purchase.

It's a good idea not to look at computer ads for at least a year after you've made your purchase because probably within hours of completing your purchase, you'll find a better computer for the same or less money. In general, expect that you'll be ready to buy another computer in three years.

Special Considerations for Laptop Computers
Chances are better than fifty-fifty your next computer purchase will be a laptop so let's look at some special laptop considerations.

Five Types of Laptops
There are basically five different laptop categories differentiated by weight, size, portability or special features:

1. **Very lightweight ultraportables**

2. **Lightweight portables**
   Both ultraportables and portables may have smaller screens and be either sparsely or fully equipped (if you pay a lot more). Less weight comes at a premium.

3. **Heavier luggables**
   These laptops are usually larger screened, less expensive and can be very powerful.

4. Tablet PCs

These computers let you enter data with a stylus, if you choose. Table PCs will become more popular as costs go down, handwriting software improves and where Windows Vista is the operating system. The new mini-tablet ultra-mobile PCs are an option.

5. Ruggedized laptops

The distinguishing feature of these computers is that they are designed to take more of a beating.

Many laptops are used as desktop substitutes. In those cases, a laptop's weight may be less of a concern for you.

Tip: Mobile Chips

If you buy a laptop, consider getting one with a *mobile chip*—a computer processing chip specifically designed for laptops. At this time, these mobile chips generally run cooler than chips initially designed for desktops (and later placed in laptops) and they usually have a longer battery life, too. The next generation of desktop chips will be designed to run cooler.

Tip: Screen Sizes and Working on Planes

If you often work on a plane, remember that laptop screens bigger than 14 or maybe 15 inches have a tough time fitting in airplane seating spaces.

Docking Stations and Port Replicators

If you're using your laptop as a desktop substitute, consider getting a docking station or a port replicator. Many of these devices can function as a stand so you can adjust the height of your laptop. They also provide additional USB ports and connections to your laptop computer for an external keyboard, mouse, printer, Ethernet or other uses.

Product Tips: Port Replicator and Docking Station

Targus AWE0501US Ergo D-Pro Desktop Notebook Stand

with Port Replicator Module. Targus, Inc., 877/482-7487 [CA] or www.targus.com

Targus ACP50US Universal Notebook Docking Station with Video. Targus, Inc., 877/482-7487 [CA] or www.targus.com

Three Ergonomic Challenges

Laptops give you much more freedom but sometimes freedom comes at an ergonomic cost.

Weight

When laptops start to weigh more than seven pounds, traveling with them can be a chore or a backbreaking experience. And that's not counting the weight of the laptop bag, adapter, extra battery, external mouse or keyboard and laptop cooling pad you may be lugging along with the laptop.

Positioning

Positioning a laptop correctly is difficult because the screen and the keyboard are attached and what may be a good ergonomic distance for the screen isn't for the keyboard. (See Chapter 16 for laptop positioning tips.)

Heat

Laptops also generate considerable heat, which can not only poten-tially fry your computer's motherboard but also burn you. Why take a chance?

Tip: Cooling Pad

Wherever you use your laptop, consider getting a laptop cooling pad (many are inexpensive) to place under your computer. If the pad plugs into your computer for power via a USB connection (rather than a separate power source), you can take the pad with you anywhere.

The Goldilocks approach—not too hot, not too cold—works with porridge and laptops. Avoid temperature extremes and fluctuations.

For example, don't leave your laptop in a hot trunk, which can cook components and screens. And an icy cold environment can crack a screen.

Batteries

Another important concern with laptops is whether your battery will last long enough before needing a recharge. Although you can always bring another extra fully-charged battery along, you may not want to carry any extra weight. Look for computers that have an instant-on feature to save battery life. Here are five other ways to maximize battery power:

1. Since your LCD screen is the biggest energy consumer on your machine, reduce the screen's brightness while working on battery power to extend battery life.

2. Because a bigger screen requires more energy, get a laptop with a screen no larger than 14 or maybe 15 inches.

3. Remove any devices that don't need to be attached (e.g., USB drives or PC cards that aren't being used) because they draw energy from your battery.

4. Increase the amount of memory (RAM) that's in your computer so your hard drive doesn't work as hard or use as much power.

5. Through your computer's operating system (e.g., Windows), adjust the power options to save energy when your computer is on but you're not using it; specify a shorter time period before the screen of your idle computer goes blank, the laptop hibernates or an inactive hard disk shuts off.

Product Tips: Battery Chargers and Adapters

APC Universal Notebook Battery can give you up to eight additional hours of battery life depending on your laptop's power, screen and other settings and weighs less than two pounds. American Power Conversion Corp., 877/800-4272 [RI] or www.apc.com

iGo EverywherePower adapters (with interchangeable tips sold separately) can recharge laptops, cellphones, PDAs and other mobile devices from auto, air and wall outlets. Mobility Electronics, Inc., 888/205-0093 [TX] or www.igo.com

ZIP-LINQ has USB cables and power adapters you can plug into the USB port of a computer to send power to handheld devices or to let the devices get power from a car's cigarette lighter or a 110-volt wall socket. ZIP-LINQ, 800/609-7550 [CA] or www.ziplinq.com

Protective Travel Cases for Your Laptop

If you're using a laptop travel case, make sure the case has plenty of shock-absorbing, air-filled pouches for padding to protect your computer if it's accidentally dropped or knocked around. But there's more to consider with a laptop bag.

Too small a bag makes it difficult to have enough protection but too large a bag may mean it's not considered carry-on luggage on a plane. Features to look for include: (a) different-sized outer pockets to hold personal items, business cards, pens, maybe even a PDA or cellphone, (b) wheels or padding in the shoulder straps to ease the work in transporting your laptop, (c) expandable bags to let you bring souvenirs and other extra items home and (d) bags with paler linings to make it easier to see the contents of the bag in dim light (such as on an airplane).

Backpack Tip

Before you buy a laptop bag, think about this. To deter laptop computer theft when you're out in public, you may want to make your laptop more inconspicuous by using an inexpensive backpack (with towels for cushioning) rather than a laptop bag.

Product Tips: Padded Cases

Belkin Corp., 877/523-5546 [CA] or www.belkin.com

Kensington Technology Group, 800/235-6708 or www.kensington.com

Targus, Inc., 877/482-7487 [CA] or www.targus.com

Computer Security on the Road

Away from your office, your computer information and equipment are more at risk. For starters, you need to avoid public settings while working on sensitive information or financial transactions with your laptop and take extra precautions when using a USB drive on someone else's computer.

USB Drives

If you're traveling light and just bringing along a USB flash drive or USB small hard drive with essential files rather than your laptop, plugging this drive into someone else's computer has the risk of leaving traces of your data on the host computer. So look for USB drives or software specially designed to mitigate this risk.

Product Tip: Protected USB Drives

The *M-Trust Drive*, as described in Chapters 2 and 13, is designed to allow mobile professionals to securely store sensitive information. It has strong hardware encryption and complex password protection and can even be set to self-destruct after too many wrong password attempts. M-Systems, Ltd., www.m-systems.com

Product Tip: USB Flash Device Protection Software

P.I. Protector Mobility Suite software, loaded on a USB flash drive, is designed to help you maintain your privacy by diverting your Internet activities to the flash drive and leaving no trace of your activities on the computer hard drive. P.I. Protector does not require installation or additional set up on the host computer. Imagine LAN, Inc., 800/372-9776 [NH] or www.imaginelan.com

Don't forget about antivirus, antispyware and software firewall protection for your USB drive (see Chapter 2).

Laptops

When you walk out the door with your laptop, make sure your computer has a software firewall, your antivirus and antispyware software is turned on and the level of wireless protection is maximized. (See Chapter 2 on VPNs and hot spots.)

To discourage others from peeking over your shoulder while you're working on sensitive or proprietary material at an airplane terminal or another public location, use smaller fonts, a lower brightness setting on your PC and if necessary, a privacy filter on your laptop's screen.

Tip: Password Protection

Make sure your laptop's password protection feature is operative. This can block others from even booting up your laptop and may show pertinent contact/reward information on your screen. Some computers go a step further by providing fingerprint or eyescan verification in order to boot up.

You can encrypt the data on your laptop (or a mobile device), use a lock on your computer or install software that lets you remotely wipe out all the data if your laptop is stolen.

For more information about protecting you and your information, see Chapters 1 through 3.

Preventing Laptop Theft

As far as preventing theft of your laptop, common sense (don't let your laptop out of your sight even in a bathroom) and basic security measures are your best first line of defense. FBI statistics show that just three percent of stolen laptop computers are recovered and that's why prevention is the best cure.

If possible, avoid using a laptop in public places such as an airport. Put a label on your laptop with your contact information and an offer of a reward for returning your computer. Make sure your laptop is covered by your insurance at any location.

Always have separate backups of essential information whether on another disk and/or through an online storage service.

Product Tips: Track-and-Recover Software

Track-and-recover software can trace a signal when your computer or mobile device is logged on to the Internet.

CyberAngel Security Software silently transmits an alert to a security monitoring center if the authentication is breached at login or boot-up. The software identifies the location from which that computer is calling. CyberAngel Security Solutions, Inc., 800/501-4344 [TN] or www.sentryinc.com

Stealth Signal software secretly sends a signal via telephone or an Internet connection allowing Stealth Signal to track your computer's location when you report it as lost or stolen. The software can also delete files remotely. Computer Security Products, Inc., 800/466-7636 [NH] or www.computersecurity.com

Helpful Laptop Accessories

A number of accessories can help make your laptop more productive. In general, if you're having trouble finding user-replaceable accessories such as batteries or rechargers for laptops or other mobile electronic devices, try Mobility Electronics, Inc. (888/205-0093 [AZ] or www.igo.com) or Targus, Inc., (877/482-7487 [CA] or www.targus.com).

Product Tips: Accessories

Monitor Screen Cleaner: *Klear Screen* is a manufacturer-recommended screen cleaner designed to safely clean screens without scratching them when used with their optical-grade Micro-Chamois or Micro-Fiber Polishing Cloths. Meridrew Enterprises, 800/505-5327 [CA] or www.klearscreen.com

Surge Protector: The *Targus PAPWR001U Mobile Notebook Surge Protector* helps safeguard your laptop computer from costly damage that can occur during power surges and spikes. Targus, Inc., 877/482-7487 [CA] or www.targus.com

Computer Buying Checklist

As discussed earlier in this chapter, how you'll use a computer determines the most important decision points for you. Of course, your budget will help you differentiate between your dream list and reality.

Use this checklist as a starting point to identify the main options to consider when you make your next purchase.

1. Manufacturer

Buy from the larger companies. Check out the leading computer magazines (e.g., *PC Magazine* and *PC World*) for their latest reviews and surveys on customer satisfaction, computer repairs and reliability data.

2. Computer chip type and speed

Although faster is better, fastest may be too expensive. There are mobile chips (which are better for laptops) and desktop-type chips. Hyper-threading chips can handle more than one process at a time. Besides the processor speed, the cache and front side bus specs help determine the overall speed (and cost) of your machine. Chips are expensive so cost may be your limiting factor here. (Some computers have security chips built in to help prevent unauthorized access to sensitive data and to help encrypt data.)

Tip: 64-bit, Multicore Chips
64-bit chips are replacing 32-bit chips and dual and other multicore chips that multiply your computer's processing power are becoming more popular and help you multitask more efficiently.

When you're calculating how much your next computer will cost, also consider compatibility costs.

Tip: Compatibility Costs and Concerns

Your existing software may not be compatible with a newer chip (e.g., a 64-bit chip). Ask about software compatibility before making your purchase. If there's a problem, you'll need to get newer versions of the software programs you regularly use (and newer versions may not be available). This incompatibility issue can also come into play if you change your computer's operating system, e.g., switching to a newer version of Windows.

See whether all of your hardware will work with the new chip or operating system. Sometimes manufacturers do not update the drivers on older equipment so maybe, for example, your older, reliable printer won't work on a newer operating system. Or a new operating system may require a faster chip, more RAM, video RAM or dedicated video RAM.

3. Operating system

If you're going to get a Windows operating system, take a look at the Windows Media Center Edition 2005 (including Update Rollup 2) to give you flexibility to make your computer part of a total digital experience, including your TV and other entertainment needs. The Media Center software will be built into some versions of Windows Vista, the successor to Windows XP.

4. Computer displays—monitors and screens

Chances are you'll get an LCD monitor with your desktop computer or have an LCD screen built into your laptop computer. Although the computer display size (number of inches) and shape (traditional or widescreen) of a screen are important, make sure the display isn't too bright or too reflective.

Images aren't static on a computer monitor or screen. They are constantly being refreshed (repainted). Different displays have different refresh rates. Too slow a refresh rate (below 75 Hz) can cause the image to flicker and lead to eyestrain and headaches.

In general, look for a refresh rate of 75 to 85 Hz.

All monitors and screens do not display changing images at the same response rate. Speed is more important for displaying not only high-end graphics and games with ever-changing fast images but also TV and DVD images. By the way, in general, the bulkier CRT monitors are better at displaying games and graphics than LCD monitors.

Tip: Lower Numbers Are Better
A 12ms response rate is faster than a 25ms rate.

If you'll want to see high definition content using the second-generations DVDs (Blu-ray or HD-DVD), check to see whether your operating system, monitor and graphics card are all HD compliant.

For maximum flexibility on connections, get a monitor that has both analog and digital connections.

See Chapter 16, Ergonomics, for helpful tips on positioning your monitor.

5. Hard disk size
Unless you want to buy a very inexpensive laptop, try to get at least 60 to 100 GB (gigabytes) for a laptop. Get a 160 to 500 GB hard drive for a desktop computer especially if you'll be storing a lot of media content. *SATA* is a newer type of hard drive and *PMR (Perpendicular Magnetic Recording)* is the newest type (potentially offering higher storage capacities). It won't be long before desktops and laptops commonly have one or multiple terabyte (1,000 gigabyte) hard drives, especially to accommodate the storage requirements of *HD* (High Definition) video.

6. Hard disk speed
Faster is better. Try to get a laptop no slower than 5400 RPM (most are 4200 RPM) and a desktop no slower than 7200 RPM, with at least a 2 MB cache.

7. **RAM (amount of memory)**

Just as chips and hard disks vary in speed, so does RAM. DDR2 is faster than DDR. With computers, more speed means more cost. Get no less than 512 MB but preferably 1 GB or more especially if you'll be using Windows Vista.

8. **Weight**

For a laptop, decide whether an ultramobile, ultraportable, portable or luggable is best for you.

9. **Battery life**

When you're looking for your next laptop computer, get a longer-lasting battery that lets you recharge at any point with no ill effect. With some batteries, you have to drain the charge completely before recharging or else you'll lose some battery capacity.

It may be a good idea to buy any user-replaceable accessories such as an extra battery close to the time you purchase a new laptop just in case they aren't available later.

10. **Optical drive**

The choices keep changing here with DVD drives replacing traditional CD drives. You can help avoid DVD drive incompatibility issues with first-generation DVD drives by getting a plus/minus drive (DVD +/-). Multi-layer DVD drives have more capacity than the older DVD drives and the new, second generation Blu-ray and HD-DVD drives are very high capacity drives that are competing to become the "standard" HD drive. Since the trend is for using DVD drives more often, get more capacity than a one-layer first generation drive.

11. **Wi-Fi and wireless broadband connections**

Bluetooth and other wireless connections are becoming standard equipment. (See Chapter 2 for Bluetooth security issues.) Get an integrated Wi-Fi card that uses the latest standards. WiMax as well as combo WiMax/Wi-Fi capabilities will become common in the not-too-distant future. Besides Wi-Fi, consider a EV-DO, EDGE or HSDPA wireless broadband access card.

Product Tips: Create Your Own Hot Spot with a Mobile Router

Junxion Box has wired and/or wireless mobile router models that let multiple computers share the Internet connection of one compatible wireless PC modem card. Junxion, Inc., www.junxion.com

KR1 Mobile Router is a wired and/or wireless mobile router that lets multiple computers share the Internet connection of a compatible wireless PC EV-DO card or compatible EV-DO phone. Kyocera Wireless Corp., www.kyocera-wireless.com

Be on the lookout for ratification of the Wi-Fi *n standard* by the Enhanced Wireless Consortium, a group of the largest wireless chip and computer equipment manufacturers. The n standard will be two to 10 times faster than earlier standards and will be able to transmit high-quality wireless and video transmissions.

12. USB and FireWire connections

Get at least three USB 2.0 ports (and maybe also one FireWire port) to connect up a keyboard, mouse, printer, external hard drive, camera and other devices to your computer. You can also always add additional USB ports with a USB hub.

13. Keyboard and mouse

An optical mouse stays cleaner and is more accurate than a roller-ball mouse. The trend is towards wireless here, too. What's more important is to get equipment that feels good to you. See Chapter 16 on ergonomics.

14. Card reader

If you're intending to connect up your camera or camcorder, see if the card reader on your computer is compatible with your equipment.

15. Included software

See whether any bundled software turns a good deal into a great one.

16. Security features

Some computers include fingerprint or eye-scanning readers, a built-in security chip or data encryption software as security features. Very often, these computer manufacturers also recommend that you use secure passwords, too.

17. Video RAM

This type of memory is most important for working with or editing graphics and images or playing higher-end games. However you're using your computer, if you're intending to get the Windows Vista operating system (and want to take advantage of all the available features), it would make sense to beef up your video RAM with dedicated memory of 64 to 128 MB or more. Separate, dedicated memory is better than shared memory, which drains off part of your RAM.

18. Built-in TV tuner

More TV viewers are seeing their shows via the Internet (IPTV — Internet Protocol television). You may want to get a computer system with a built-in TV tuner.

Product Tips: Remote Viewing

Orb gives you access to your digital media (photos, video and music) from your remote computer or Web-enabled mobile devices. If your PC has a TV tuner, you can watch live or recorded TV. Video quality depends on available bandwidth. Other uses include monitoring your home or office by accessing your webcam from anywhere in the world, getting driving directions and maps when you are on the go and checking weather and stocks anytime, anywhere. Orb Networks, Inc., www.orb.com

Slingbox lets you watch your cable, satellite TV or digital video recorder (DVR) programming on your computer anywhere in the world using an Internet broadband connection and one of the following: (a) an Ethernet connection, (b) a Powerline Ethernet adapter for standard electrical outlets or (c) a 54 Mbps wireless game adapter. At the time this book is being written, there is also a

beta version for network-enabled mobile devices using
Windows Mobile. Sling Media, Inc.,
www.slingmedia.com

19. Warranty

Find out the number of years, what's included or excluded,
the waiting time for service and whether it's on-site or carry-in
(or mail-in) service. There are also no-fault warranties that
cover you if you drop or damage your computer—check out
the fine print on this. If a three-year warranty is too expensive,
see whether your credit card company will automatically
double a one-year warranty at no extra cost if you use the
credit card for the purchase. Before buying a refurbished
computer, see whether the free extended warranty applies
here, too.

20. Cost

No matter where you start, it always comes back to money and
budgets.

21. Return policy

Especially if you're ordering a laptop that you haven't personally tried out, find out how long the trial period is (if there is
one) and what you'll be charged (e.g., a restocking fee and/or a
shipping fee) if you return the computer.

Don't forget to buy a high-quality surge protector, too.

The Next Step

To see the most current specifications, go to the websites of two major
computer manufacturers and go through a mock online purchase to
see the options available for customizing a system. Very often the
sites include explanations of the various options.

Since we all depend on at least one mobile device in addition to our
computers, read the next chapter so you can identify the right mobile
device features for you.

18

Mobile
Devices

There used to be more certainty and clarity in the world. Back in the 1980s when personal computers became essential equipment, a phone was just a phone, you didn't get charged for water in a restaurant and when someone asked if you liked salsa, it just meant a sauce and not an invitation to dance. Times have changed.

Or have they? If Shakespeare were living today, he'd be writing: "What's in a name? That which we call a mobile device by any other name would be as sweet." Bottom line, you can't go by what anything, especially a mobile device, is called to know what it really is or does.

Here's just a sampling of the wide variety of mobile devices and names: BlackBerry, cellphone, smartphone, PDA, Pocket PC, smartwatch, video iPod, smart sunglasses (which have phones), GPS cellphones for children and seniors (Wherify, Inc., www.wherifywireless.com) and the PetsCell (the first cellphone optimized for animals that allows owners to talk to their pets and use GPS technology to track lost pets, PetsMobility, Inc., www.petsmobility.com). Laptop computers are sometimes put in the mobile device category, too, but not in this book.

Sites such as Google offer personalized homepages for mobile devices to let you do Web searches, check email, news, stocks and other info from one central page (www.google.com—click the *Personalized Home* link). Software such as *Opera Mobile* and *Opera Mini* are making full Internet browsing a reality on most mobile devices (www.opera.com).

Mobile devices (sometimes called mobile handheld devices) are undergoing tremendous change with features morphing and converging and being added all the time.

Mobile Device Capabilities

When you look at a mobile device, you need to see whether it really is one or more of the following:

- Cellphone

- Internet browser

- Email, IM and text messaging communications tool

- PDA (personal digital assistant)

- Organizer

- Calendar

- Computer (with hard disk storage, access to your software applications and the ability to display presentations)

- Camera (not only to take photos but also to get information without using your keyboard—e.g., with the *mobile visual search technique,* you can take a photo of a movie billboard, send the photo to a database and receive the movie trailer or buy tickets)

- Video camcorder

- Digital audio player

- Digital video player

- TV (to watch *mobisodes*—mobile TV episodes)

- Internet radio

- GPS (Global Positioning System)

- Navigation device

- Business card scanner

- Voice/memo recorder with voice recognition to type emails and text messages and perform spoken commands

- Game machine

- Dictation transcriber

- Pager

Mobile Device Trend and Warning

In the past, mobile devices were not as powerful and they were a companion device to a personal computer. Today, the trend is for mobile devices to be phones and also take on more of the power and capability of computers (and mini-entertainment centers). Over time, these small devices coupled with a projection of a full-size virtual keyboard on a desk or other surface may replace your laptop computer. The downside is that as more cellphones and other telephone-enabled mobile devices link to the Internet, the risk of cellphone viruses and other malware increases. Antivirus software will help prevent problems.

So who needs a mobile device today? The more complex and demanding your life and career become, the more you need the time management, productivity and communication tools offered by these devices. The bottom line, if you're like most people, is that you just don't walk out the door these days without taking at least one mobile device along.

Selecting the Right Mobile Device(s)

What's so great about today's mobile devices is that at least one of them will function the way you want to work. You have more choice and flexibility today when selecting and customizing the features you need. (Remember, though, not to feel guilty if you don't use each and every feature that comes with a device—use only what you need.)

The key is to identify which device(s) will most easily *adapt to your workstyle and lifestyle*. There are three rules of thumb (and "thumb" is an important word when it comes to mobile devices): (1) look for the *essential* features, not the total number of features, (2) consider ease of use and (3) remember, the *fewer* the number of devices you have, the better.

Identify the Basics You Need

What basics do you want your mobile device to do? Organize contacts? Calendar your work schedule? Handle email? Send instant messages? Make cellphone calls? Wi-Fi calls? VoIP calls? Let you take notes? Search the Web with a fully-functioning Web browser? Attach a photo to a contact's name? Use your voice to type text? Record video? Let you arrange and participate in online meetings?

Intuitive or Complex?

On some devices, the software is intuitive and easy to use while on others it's just too complex. If you know you'll never open a manual, find a device that performs the essential functions for you in an accessible, intuitive way.

Product Tip: The Simple Cellphone

Vodafone Simply is a cellphone *without* the bells and whistles. If you can operate your answering machine, you can handle this cellphone. For example, to pick up messages, you just push the Message button that has a picture of a phone. At the time this book is being written, it's being sold around the world but not yet in the U.S. So be on the lookout for this phone if simpler is better for you when it comes to technology. Vodafone Group, plc, www.vodafone.com

Five Basic Criteria for Selecting a Mobile Device

Coming up shortly is an extensive mobile device checklist. But first, on a very simple level, consider these five basic selection criteria:

1. Size

What's the right one for you?

2. Features

Which features do you need? Phone, email, Web searching, contact management, organizing features? More advanced features?

3. Accessibility

How easy is it to find information using the device?

4. Compatibility

How easy is it to use the device with your computer and its software (such as PIMs, personal information manager software)? If you have a mobile device and a computer using the same software program (e.g., a personal information manager), make sure it works on both.

5. Looks, image and appeal

What is appropriate for your position and lifestyle?

Mobile Device Checklist

How do you determine which is the right mobile device for you? Ask the right questions and you'll get the right answers. Determine which of the following are must-haves:

1. Number of tools

Will one mobile device meet all or most of your important needs (phone, email, instant or text messaging, the Web, calendar, word processing) or will it take multiple tools to handle your needs?

> ### Warning: Don't Look for Info in Too Many Places
> Don't store your digital information in too many places; otherwise, you may have different versions of your information and may need to sync it (see #11 below).

2. Features and multifunctionality

Before you buy is the time to see how much you can do with the mobile device. Look for the ability to:

- Make phone calls (with hands-free dialing and speakerphone)
- Perform essential functions based on voice recognition alone
- Handle personal and corporate email
- Transfer and/or accept files as attachments to emails
- Send and receive instant messages, SMS (text messages) and MMS (graphics, videos and sound files)
- Search the Web (in a limited way or with a fully-functioning Web browser) at possibly high-data speeds (HSPDA) similar to fixed-line broadband speeds
- Easily create a calendar, to-do list and master list for appointments, recurring tasks, projects and other to-dos
- Have audible reminders
- Access specific PIM information about contacts (such as phone numbers and email addresses), products and services
- Use scaled back or full versions of word processing, spreadsheet, presentation and other software
- Have navigational tools and directories of restaurants and movie theaters via GPS
- Use a built-in camera or video camcorder

Explore all the potential already built into the mobile device you own. Do you know that your phone may not need an Internet connection to do some online searching at services such as Google? If your phone can do text messaging, you can send a text message (SMS—Short Message Service) query such as "weather Chicago" to the phone number 46645 (which is number talk for "GOOGL") and then get a text reply from Google with no links and no Web pages. (See Chapter 7 for more on this Google SMS capability.)

Tip: Mobile Search Services

Google also has a Mobile Web search service (www.google.com/xhtml) that only links to pages that are formatted to display properly on the small screens of devices with a Web browser. Google has another mobile search service (www.google.com/wml) for phones that don't have a Web browser but do have WML (wireless markup language). Google and other providers are expanding the content and search services for mobile devices.

Tip: Full Web Access for Dumb Phones

But wait, there's more. It used to be that only smartphones could browse the Web. Now there's *Opera Mini*, a fast and easy alternative that allows users to access the Web on mobile phones that would normally be incapable of running a Web browser. This includes the vast majority of today's WAP-enabled phones. Instead of requiring the phone to process Web pages, it uses a remote server to pre-process the page before sending it to the phone. This makes Opera Mini perfect for phones with very low resources or low bandwidth connections. Opera Software, ASA, www.opera.com/products/mobile/operamini

3. Cellphone features

In addition to nonphone features such as email, instant and text messaging and Internet capability, useful cellphone features include:

- Easy-to-read display with large enough fonts

- Large enough keys to punch in numbers and type text

- One-hand operation for the phone functions

- Caller ID (and on flip phones, an external screen caller ID so you know who is calling before deciding to open the cover)

- Voice dialing

- *Full*-duplex speakerphone (with *half*-duplex speaker-phones, only one person can speak at a time; if one person is speaking, the other one can't be heard until the first person stops)

- Call forwarding

- Call waiting

- Conference calling

- Recalling last numbers dialed

- Walkie-talkie push button talking, if needed

- Large enough phone number storage capacity

- Loud enough ringer that's easy to hear

- Bluetooth and infrared connections so you can use a headset and connect up wirelessly to other devices and computers

- Camera, video recorder, MP3, radio and video capability, if needed

- *Convergence* where you roam seamlessly between mobile and Wi-Fi networks

- *GSM* (global system for mobile communications) digital technology if you travel abroad, especially to Europe or *UMA* (phones that combine GSM and *wlan*, wireless capabilities)

- Compatibility between your phone and your carrier's network

4. Size, weight and portability of the tool

Make sure it's a good fit. How big is too big? How small is small enough? As devices become smaller, it's easier to lose them.

5. Screen size, resolution and clarity

For mobile devices, as the screen size gets smaller, it limits your ability to read lengthier emails and documents. Can the font size be adjusted to make information more readable? Color screens are more readable than black-and-white ones.

Test out a screen to see if it has a high enough resolution. Then go outside in sunlight and see whether the screen is still readable.

6. Battery life

Find out how long your device will work before needing a recharge (try to get three or more hours of talk time) and how long it will take to recharge. Make sure you won't lose your data if the device runs out of power.

Product Tip: Emergency Battery Recharger

Sidewinder is a hand-crank recharger that is easy to use and gives a charge to your cellphone even if the power is out. Check for compatibility with your device. IST, www.istdesigns.com

In the not-too-distant future, batteries may be replaced by hydrogen/oxygen fuel cells.

7. Keyboard/data entry

See if it's easy to write in or key in data. Is there a virtual keyboard? Is there a stylus or built-in keyboard with the device? What is the keyboard like? Is it the usual QWERTY keyboard? How small (or big) are the keys? Are they large enough to be usable? If not, consider having an external keyboard to connect to your mobile device if it allows such a connection. There are portable keyboards that fold up into a very small size but they usually just work with specific models of mobile devices. Does the device include software that anticipates and completes words to cut down on your typing?

Product Tip: Foldup Keyboards

Stowaway Keyboards are wireless, small foldup keyboards. There are different keyboards designed for the major mobile operating systems. Think Outside Corp., www.thinkoutside.com

8. Operating system

The operating system you select can affect compatibility and synchronization issues. Is the operating system so widely used you'll be able to easily find new hardware add-ons and new software applications as time goes on? Will the operating system work with your email program or just a proprietary email program from the system maker?

9. Processor speed

Just as with a computer, it may be worth it to have a faster machine to do your tasks.

10. Flexibility/connecting other devices

If you think at some point you may be adding memory, hard drives or other peripherals, applications and tools, see what's involved. Does your device use an operating system that limits or welcomes products and applications created by outside vendors? How are other add-on devices connected? Via USB 1.1? USB 2.0? Some other way?

Product Tip: Systems to Merge Cellphones and Landlines

Dock-N-Talk supports over 700 cellphone models and lets you dock your cellphone and use a corded or cordless phone to make and receive your cellphone calls. Phone Labs Technology Co., www.phonelabs.com

The *RCA Cell Docking System* (model #23200RE3) lets you make and receive cellular phone calls anywhere in your home or office using your cellphone or the included RCA cordless telephone. One benefit is that you can use your cellphone's long distance minutes while talking on the RCA cordless handset. Your cellphone is placed in the docking station, while the cordless handset can be plugged into any electrical outlet. You can switch between using your cellphone minutes and the landline just by pressing a button on the cordless handset that says Home or Cell. The device is designed to add a virtual second line so you can fax on one line and talk on the other. Check for compatibility with your cellphone model. Thomson, www.rca.com

11. Synchronization of devices

If you keep your information on a mobile device and also on a computer, another mobile device or the Web, you better have the same information on all of them through *synchronization*. Easy synchronization is very important because if it's a pain to do it, you may be inclined to put it off. You don't want to miss an important meeting or telephone appointment because different appointment schedules were stored in different places.

Synchronization may involve updating one device at a time, several at the same time or each device automatically receiving the latest information each time it's turned on. Also your mobile device may let you drag and drop files to a computer without having to go through the entire data synchronization process. Synchronization may be available through wireless (and cradleless) synchronization via Wi-Fi, Bluetooth or other technologies.

Product Tips: Mobile Device Contact Manager and Synchronization Programs

You may need programs to stay in touch with your contacts and keep their information synchronized on your mobile device and computer.

ACT! by Sage, as more fully described in Chapter 11, is a powerful, award-winning, easy-to-use contact and customer management program with synchronization capability. Sage Software, 877/501-4496 [CA] or www.act.com

GoldMine, as more fully described in Chapter 11, is a top-rated contact manager program loaded with features including synchronization. FrontRange Solutions, 800/776-7889 [CA] or www.goldmine.com

CompanionLink Software, Inc. is a leading provider of synchronization solutions for PDAs and handheld organizers as well as ASP providers (companies that offer software applications and related services over the Internet). The company offers synchronization solutions for ACT!, GoldMine, Lotus Notes and Microsoft Outlook and is compatible with Pocket PC, Palm OS and BlackBerry wireless handheld devices. CompanionLink Software, Inc., 800/386-1623 [OR] or www.companionlink.com

Documents To Go Total Office lets you synchronize and work with your Microsoft Word, Excel, PowerPoint and Access files along with your Outlook data using a Palm-powered handheld or smartphone (such as the Treo 650 smartphone) or the LifeDrive mobile manager. DataViz, www.dataviz.com

12. Storage/memory capacity

Determine how much storage you need. Some mobile devices have substantial built-in memory and even hard disks as well as the capacity to connect additional storage devices.

13. Accessing and receiving data

Think about whether all the data you'll need will be on the device or whether you'll need to access other sources such as your main computer.

Can you connect the device to the Internet, your computer, your company's intranet or VPN (virtual private network) and essential websites (such as online banking) and have adequate access to needed data and information?

Product Tip: Mobile Website Content

AvantGo is a free service that lets you download news and other content from mobile websites through syncing, wireless surfing or a combination of both. With the software, you can get thousands of specially formatted websites on your smartphone or PDA to see news, weather, sports, stock quotes, maps, movie listings and more. iAnywhere Solutions, Inc., www.avantgo.com

If you're connecting a mobile device to someone else's computer (to edit and/or print documents), see whether you can open the files directly from your device without copying them onto someone else's computer to keep the documents private. (See

Chapter 2 for security issues and solutions.)

Find out if you can have real-time access to not just your email but also your calendar, contacts and data. Does your device use *push technology* where email and other information is automatically sent to the device rather than requiring you to take steps to receive it?

Also find out how many email accounts you can access with your device and the available service packages.

14. Web access

Smaller devices may be more limited in their website accessibility. Websites often need to customize their content for a particular device so that the site content is readable by the device. This limited Web accessibility is changing. (See *Opera Mini* above.)

15. Access speed to the Internet

Before you buy, see the speed of the Internet connection. Not all devices and Web services are created equally when it comes to searching the Web, handling email and downloading and uploading files. Your speed will depend on the device's capability as well as how you're connecting to the Internet.

16. Multiple, simultaneous connections and wireless technology transfers

Give some thought as to how you'll use the device now and down the line. Can you use the phone and Wi-Fi capabilities of the device at the same time? Can your device automatically switch from using a wireless connection to using a cell connection and vice versa? Almost half of all cell calls are made from inside a building. If a phone could switch from a cell to a Wi-Fi connection, you could save money on calls.

17. Range/coverage area

Find out the short- and long-range geographic limitations for using your device and accessing data. If you're a world traveler, find out the global coverage so you know (a) in how many countries you can voice roam, access data services and make phone calls and (b) whether the cost is prohibitive. *UMA* (Unlicensed Mobile Access) phones can handle both GSM cellular technology (the most popular standard for mobile phones in the world) and wlan (Wi-Fi technology).

18. Type of connection

Find out how many types of connections (Bluetooth, Wi-Fi or some other wireless communication connection) are available and how much (or little) security is provided with each type of connection.

19. Backup

See how easy (or difficult) it is to back up essential information.

Product Tip: Cellphone Backup Devices

Cell-Stik looks like a USB thumb drive but the big difference is that it lets you back up your cellphone contacts and/or transfer them from one cellphone to another or to your computer. One end of the device has the usual USB connector (to connect up to your computer if necessary) and the other end has a cellphone adapter. You may need to have separate CellStiks for each cellphone and use your computer as an intermediary to transfer your data. Check for compatibility with your phones. Spark Technology Corp., www.sparktech .com

20. Hard-copy capability

Find out the steps to produce hard-copy output of calendars, to-do lists, contact information and other data.

21. Security to restrict turning the device on

Security is always a concern. Is there password protection, fingerprint recognition or some other system to restrict who can turn on the device?

22. Security to restrict access to data

How secure are your data and communications from the eyes

and ears of outsiders? Are encryption capabilities built in? Can you wirelessly wipe out data if a device is lost or stolen?

The more sophisticated mobile devices have always-on wireless connections and that means there's more of a chance to catch a virus or worm or suffer data theft than with plain vanilla cellphones. Since Bluetooth is not always a secure form of communication, make sure you're using all of the built-in security features if you're using Bluetooth technology. Change default passwords on wireless headsets at least quarterly. Be sure to read Chapter 2 for other Bluetooth security suggestions.

Product Tips: Mobile Device Malware Protection

For software to help protect against mobile device malware threats, try:

F-Secure Corp., www.f-secure.com

McAfee, Inc., www.mcafee.com

23. Looks, image and appeal

Think about what is appropriate for your position and lifestyle.

24. Your technology comfort level and time commitment

How comfortable you are learning new technology and how simple or complex the device is to operate may affect your purchase decision. Think about how much time it will take for you to learn how to operate the device.

25. Cost

See if your budget can afford all the features you want. Take into account not only the initial cost but the ongoing monthly charges (including data charges) for those features.

Product Tips: Free Directory Assistance

One way to save money with cellphones is to use either *800-411-METRO* or *800-FREE-411* to get free directory assistance.

Once you determine which affordable device offers what you need, give it a trial spin. If a device passes your initial in-store navigation test, get a limited (e.g., 15-day), money-back free trial to really test it out.

Product Tips: Places to Donate or Sell Old Cellphones and PDAs

If you decide to replace a phone or PDA, you can sell or donate your old mobile devices at these websites:

CollectiveGood recycles cellphones, pagers and PDAs. CollectiveGood, Inc., www.collectivegood.com

Oldcellphone buys old cellphones and also helps groups conduct recycled cellphone fundraisers for their organizations. Oldcellphone.com, www.oldcellphone.com

Ripmobile buys old cellphones for reuse or recycling. It's postage-free to send in your phone and you receive gift certificates from major companies in exchange for your phone. CollectiveGood, Inc., www.ripmobile.com

Reminder on Removing Data from Mobile Devices You're Donating

Just as a donated or recycled computer needs to have its data destroyed before coming into the hands of a stranger, the same is true for the data in mobile devices (your phone book, incoming and outgoing phone calls and text messages, stored credit card numbers, photos, memos and other information). First, remove your SIM card that has much of your data if you want to transfer that data to another device. Then, you'll need to do a series of manual reset commands to erase other data and settings. Check the manual for your phone for the correct procedure for your model or if you're having difficulty (or want to see a doublecheck of the correct steps), go to ReCellular's site at *www.wirelessrecycling.com/home/data_eraser/default.asp* and click on the manufacturer and model of your device to get instructions.

It feels good that the last topic in the book deals with recycling.

Our goal was to put together the best and latest tips, strategies and products to let you zero in on the solutions you need to know right now. We'll have met that goal if you can now make technology dance to your tune.

Index

A

268 Teach Your Computer to Dance

VoIP (continued)
  911 and, 95
  restrictions on, 75
  security issues and, 96
  spit, 94
  video calling, 94
  virtual phone numbers, 94-95
Vonage, 94
VPN
  benefits of, 34-36
  encryption and, 43
  HotSpot VPN and, 34-35
  mobile devices and, 258
  Realm MPS and, 35
  Total Net Shield and, 35

W
War driving, 7
Warranty, 246
Watson 2.0, 128
Web
  bookmarking and, 111
  browsers
    Firefox, 11
    Internet Explorer, 111
    Mozilla, 111
    NetCaptor, 111
    Opera, 111
  browser safety rankings, 107
  cookies and, 18-19, 106-107
  definition of, 104
  difference between Internet and, 103-104
  multiple windows for searching on, 111-112
  RSS feeds, 112-114
  searching, 103-148
  spyware and, 6-8, 17-18, 36, 51-52
  tabbed browsing and, 110-111
  viruses and, 8, 31, 38, 49, 70, 82, 131

Web conferencing
  bandwidth and, 201
  features of, 201
  GoToMeeting and, 202
  Microsoft Office Live Meeting and, 202
  mimioBoard and, 203
  mimio Xi and, 203
  NetMeeting and, 202
  software for, 202-203
  virtual meetings and, 200-201
  WebEx Meeting Center and, 203
  whiteboarding and, 202
Webex Communications, Inc., 196, 203, 207
WebEx Meeting Center, 203, 207
Web Eyes, 114
Web feeds, 113
Web information managers, 126-128
  Blinkx.tv, 126-127
  Clusty, 127
  Groxis, 127
  Internet Research Scout, 127
  Mass Downloader, 127
  Metaproducts Inquiry, 128
  Offline Explorer, 128
  Onfolio, 128
  SurfSaver, 128
  Watson 2.0, 128
Weblogs (see *blogs*)
Web page updating software
  Copernic Tracker, 129
Webpedia, 137
Webroot Software, Inc., 51
Web's Biggest, 120
Web's Biggest, LLC, 120
Web search (see *Searching the Web*)
Website safety certifications, 105
  BBBOnline, 105
  TRUSTe, 105
Web 2.0, 138-139
  Community search sites and, 139
WEP, 41

Notes

Notes

Book Description of
Baby Boomer Retirement
by

Don Silver

Every day 10,000 baby boomers are turning age 60 and another 10,000 are turning age 50.

There are going to be two groups of baby boomers at retirement age—those who prepared and those who should have.

Whether it's planning to help your parents, your children or yourself, you need a copy of *Baby Boomer Retirement: 65 Simple Ways to Protect Your Future.*

Baby Boomer Retirement is a one-stop resource for busy boomers who want to take control of their financial lives and protect their children, their parents and their financial future.

Besides planning for retirement, the book also covers a wealth of other topics including the right and wrong ways to save for a child's college education and issues dealing with marriage, remarriage, moving to a new state, taking care of your parents and improving the quality of your life.

"Astute and provocative."
—*Los Angeles Times*

"This book is the ultimate gift for a baby boomer."
—Cynthia Boman Thompson, Certified Financial Planner

"*Baby Boomer Retirement* is the right book at the right time. It responds to this generation's heightened sensitivity to its imminent responsibility with intelligence, good humor and solid advice."
—*Business Review*

Available from
www.adams-hall.com

Book Description of
Cookin' the Book$
by

Don Silver

Cookin' the Book$: Say Pasta La Vista to Corporate Accounting Tricks & Fraud is unlike any other book you've read. It's a novel about the accounting scandals with a compelling story line and great content.

"*Cookin' the Book$* stands alone as one of the funniest and straightforward works on business ethics in corporate America today."
—Peter McGuire Wolf, PhD

"The quality of the book is excellent."
—Ken Milani, Professor of Accountancy, University of Notre Dame

"What an ingenious way to communicate ethical principles! *Cookin' the Book$* is a great story. It's easy to lose yourself in the dialogue and relationship between the characters and to forget that you're learning something! Great book! I loved it!"
—Mark S. Putnam, President, Character Training Inc. and author of *Ethics for a Modern Workforce* and *Ethics for Success*

"I am always on the lookout for outstanding books. *Cookin' the Book$* is very creative and a very good read."
—Mary Feeney Bonawitz, PhD, CPA; Assistant Professor of Professional Accountancy, Penn State University-Capital College; President, American Society of Women Accountants

"*Cookin' the Book$* manages to make complicated issues crystal clear and be hilariously funny at the same time."
—Marina v.N. Whitman, Professor of Business Administration and Public Policy, University of Michigan

Available from
www.adams-hall.com

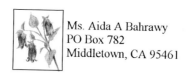

Ms. Aida A Bahrawy
PO Box 782
Middletown, CA 95461

Book Description of

The Generation Y Money Book

by

Don Silver

If you were born between 1977 and 1988, you need this book to learn how to take charge of your money. With most chapters one to two pages long, *The Generation Y Money Book: 99 Smart Ways to Handle Money* is a short, easy-to-read, step-by-step guide that's readily accessible. No other book is directed at the specific needs of your generation and written this way.

Knowing how to handle money is a skill that Gen Yers need for life. Yet chances are neither your schools nor your parents had the ability *and* made the effort to teach it. *The Generation Y Money Book* fills that gap with 99 smart ways to handle money.

Chapters cover "Money-Smart Ways" to think about money, live day-to-day, shop, work, handle debt and credit, deal with financial institutions, handle paperwork, make money grow and more.

"*The Generation Y Money Book* is excellent! The book is extremely well written. Great book."
— Cheryl D. Jennings, Ph.D., Gus A. Stavros Center for Economic Education, Florida State University

"It's well-written. What an ideal birthday present!"
— William C. Wood, Center for Economic Education, James Madison University

"*The Generation Y Money Book* should be found on every shelf of every college and community library."
— Midwest Book Review

Available from
www.adams-hall.com

Book Description of

Organized to Be Your Best!
Transforming How You Work

by

Susan Silver

This is the one book you need to get control over your desk, your computer and your demanding work life. Rely on the "bible of organization" and you'll see how to:

o Control multiple, ever-changing projects and priorities, 24x7 work schedules and information overload

o Manage email, instant and text messages, phone calls and other communications

o Devise a time and information system just for you

o Work more collaboratively with others in person and online

o Master a messy desk as you learn to turn piles into files

o Maximize all your workspaces wherever they're located

o Get the most from your computer and mobile devices and protect yourself in the process

Suan Silver is the recognized organizing expert and bestselling author of the award-winning bible of organization *Organized to Be Your Best!* and the coauthor of *Teach Your Computer to Dance.*

Ms. Silver is a knowledgeable, entertaining and hands-on training and coaching professional who heads the company Positively Organized!

Available from
www.adams-hall.com